BRAIN
BOOT CAMP

Thunder Bay Press

An imprint of Printers Row Publishing Group

10350 Barnes Canyon Road, Suite 100, San Diego, CA 92121

www.thunderbaybooks.com • mail@thunderbaybooks.com

Correspondence regarding the content of this book should be addressed to Thunder Bay Press, Editorial Department, at the above address. Author and rights inquiries should be addressed to Carlton Books Ltd, 20 Mortimer Street, London, W1T 3JW, United Kingdom.

Publisher: Peter Norton
Associate Publisher: Ana Parker
Publishing/Editorial Team: April Farr, Kelly Larsen, Kathryn C. Dalby
Editorial Team: JoAnn Padgett, Melinda Allman, Dan Mansfield

ISBN: 978-1-68412-940-9

All images: © iStockphoto & Shutterstock

Printed in Dubai

23 22 21 20 19 2 3 4 5 6

BRAIN
BOOT CAMP

Tantalize and train your brain with
more than 350 baffling puzzles

Tim Dedopulos &
British Mensa

THUNDER BAY
P·R·E·S·S
San Diego, California

CONTENTS

INTRODUCTION

INTRODUCTION

Puzzles are as old as humankind. It's inevitable – it's the way we think. Our brains make sense of the world around us by looking at the pieces that combine to make up our environment. Each piece is then compared to everything else we have encountered. We compare it by shape, size, colour, textures, a thousand different qualities, and place it into the mental categories it seems to belong to. Then also consider other nearby objects, and examine what we know about them, to give context. We keep on following this web of connections until we have enough understanding of the object of our attention to allow us to proceed in the current situation. We may never have seen a larch before, but we can still identify it as a tree. Most of the time, just basic recognition is good enough, but every time we perceive an object, it is cross-referenced, analysed, pinned down – puzzled out.

This capacity for logical analysis – for reason – is one of the greatest tools in our mental arsenal, on a par with creativity and lateral induction. Without it, science would be non-existent, and mathematics no more than a shorthand for counting items. In fact, although we might have made it out of the caves, we wouldn't have got far.

Furthermore, we automatically compare ourselves to each other – we place ourselves in mental boxes along with everything else. We like to know where we stand. It gives us an instinctive urge to compete, both against our previous bests and against each other. Experience, flexibility and strength are acquired through pushing personal boundaries, and that's as true of the mind as it is of the body. Deduction is something that we derive satisfaction and worth from, part of the complex blend of factors that goes into making up our self-image. We get a very pleasurable sense of achievement from succeeding at something, particularly if we suspected it might be too hard for us.

The brain gives meaning and structure to the world through analysis, pattern recognition, and logical deduction – and our urge to measure and test ourselves is an unavoidable reflex that results from that. So what could be more natural than spending time puzzling?

The dawn of puzzling

The urge to solve puzzles appears to be a universal human constant. They can be found in every culture, and in every time that we have good archaeological evidence for. The earliest material uncovered so far that is indisputably a puzzle has been dated to a little after 2000 BC – and the first true writing we know of only dates back to 2600 BC. The puzzle text is recorded on a writing tablet, preserved from ancient Babylonia. It is a mathematical puzzle based around working out the sides of a triangle.

Other puzzles from around the same time have also been discovered. The Rhind Papyrus from ancient Egypt describes a puzzle that is almost certainly a precursor of the traditional English riddle "As I Was Going to St. Ives." In the Rhind Papyrus, a puzzle is constructed around the clearly unreal situation of seven houses, each containing seven cats – and every cat kills seven mice that themselves had each consumed seven ears of millet.

In a similar foreshadowing, a set of very early puzzle jugs – Phoenician work from around 1700 BC, found in Cyprus – echo designs that were to become popular in medieval Europe. These particular jugs, belonging to a broad category known as Askoi, had to be filled from the bottom.

This form of trick vessel would later become known as a Cadogan Teapot. These devices have no lid, and have to be filled through a hole in the base. Because the hole funnels to a point inside the vessel, it can be filled to about half-way without spilling when it is turned back upright.

Earlier finds do exist, but so much context is lost down through the years that it can be difficult to be certain that the creators were thinking of puzzles specifically, or just of mathematical demonstrations. A set of ancient Babylonian tablets showing geometric progressions – mathematical sequences – is thought to be from 2300 BC. One of the very first mathematical finds though, thought to possibly be from as far back as 2700 BC, is a set of stone balls carved into the shapes of the Platonic solids. These are regular convex polyhedrons – three-dimensional solid shapes made up solely of identical regular polygons. The most familiar is the basic cube, made up of six squares, but there are just four others – the tetrahedron, made up of four equilateral triangles; the octahedron, made up of eight equilateral triangles; the dodecahedron, made from twelve pentagons, and the icosahedron, made of twenty equilateral triangles.

There's no way now of knowing whether the carvings were teaching aids, puzzle or game tools, demonstrations of a theory, artistic constructions or even religious icons. The fact they exist at all however shows that someone had previously spent time working out a significant abstract mathematical puzzle – discovering which regular convex polyhedrons could exist.

The first great labyrinth

One of the greatest physical puzzles ever engineered comes from the same time period. The Egyptian Pharaoh Amenemhet III constructed a funerary pyramid with a huge temple complex around it in the form of an incredible labyrinth. Designed to guard the Pharaoh's mummy and treasures from disturbance or robbery, the labyrinth was so lavish and cunning that it is said to have been both the inspiration and template for the famous labyrinth that Daedalus built at Knossos for King Minos of Crete – the one that supposedly contained the Minotaur.

A history of puzzling

Coming forward in time, the evidence for the variety and complexity of puzzles gets ever stronger – an inevitable fact of archaeological and historical research. Greek legend claims that numbered dice were invented at the siege of Troy around 1200 BC. We know that there was a craze for lateral thinking puzzles and logical dilemmas in the Greek culture from the 5th to 3rd centuries BC. A lot of very important mathematical work also took place in Greece from the middle of the first millennium BC, moving across to Rome during the first centuries AD. At the same time, the Chinese were playing with numerical puzzles and oddities, most famously the magic square, which they called Lo Shu (River Map), and also doing more strong mathematical work.

Puzzles and puzzle-like games that survive through to modern times get more common as we get closer to modern times, naturally. The game of Go arose in China some time around 500 BC, spreading to Japan a thousand years later – it is still an important sport there. At the same time, Chess was first appearing, either in India

(Chaturanga), China (Xiang-qi), or both. Puzzle rings that you have to find out how to separate also appeared in China, possibly in the 3rd century AD, as did Snakes & Ladders, around AD 700.

The first known reference to a game played with cards is in AD 969, in records reporting the activities of the Chinese Emperor Mu-tsung. These are not thought to be the playing cards now familiar in the West, however – it seems likely that those arose in Persia during the 11th or 12th century AD. The physical puzzle Solitaire is first reported in 1697. As the 18th century gave way to the 19th, the forces of the industrial revolution really started to transform the way that ideas propagated, and the puzzle world exploded.

Some of the more notable highlights include the invention of the jigsaw puzzle by John Spilsbury in 1767; Tic-Tac-Toe's first formal discussion in 1820, by Charles Babbage; poker first appearing around 1830 in the USA; Lucas inventing the Tower of Hanoi puzzle in 1883; the first crossword appearing in *New York World* on December 21, 1913, created by Arthur Wynne; Erno Rubik's invention of his Cube in 1974; and

the invention of Sudoku in 1979 for Dell Magazines by Howard Garns, an American who first called it "Number Place."

Good for the brain?

It turns out that it's a good thing puzzles are such an important part of the human psyche. Recent advances in the scientific fields of neurology and cognitive psychology have hammered home the significance of puzzles and mental exercise like never before.

We now understand that the brain continually builds, shapes and organises itself all through our lives. It is the only organ to be able to do so. Previously, we had assumed that the brain was constructed to optimise infant development, but the truth is that it continually rewrites its own operating instructions. It can route around physical damage, maximise its efficiency in dealing with commonly encountered situations and procedures, and alter its very structure in response to our experiences. This incredible flexibility is referred to as plasticity.

The most important implication of plasticity is that our mental abilities and cognitive fitness can be exercised at any age. Just like the muscles of the body, our minds can respond to exercise, allowing us to be more retentive and mentally fitter. Our early lives are the most important time, of course. Infants develop almost twice as many synapses – the mental connections that are the building-blocks of the mind – as we retain as adults, to make sure that every experience can be learnt from and given its own space in the developing mental structure. The first 36 months are particularly vital, the ones which will shape the patterns of our intellect, character and socialisation for life. A good education through to adulthood – stretching the brain right through childhood – is one of the strongest indicators of late-life mental health, particularly when followed with a mentally challenging working life.

Just as importantly however, there is little difference between the brain at the age of 25 and the age of 75. As time passes, the brain optimises itself for the lifestyle we feed it. Circuits that are hardly ever used get re-adapted to offer greater efficiency in tasks we regularly use. Just as our body maximises available energy by removing muscle we don't use, the brain removes mental tone we're never stretching – and in the same way that working out can build up muscle, so mental exercise can restore a "fit" mind.

Puzzle solving and brain growth

A surprising amount of mental decline in elders is now thought to be down to insufficient mental exercise. Where severe mental decline occurs, it is usually linked to the tissue damage of Alzheimer's Disease – although there is now even evidence that strong mental exercise lets the brain route around even Alzheimer's damage, lessening impairment. In other cases, where there is no organic damage, the main cause is disuse. Despite old assumptions, we do not significantly lose huge swathes of brain cells as we age. Better still, mental strength that has been allowed to atrophy may be rebuilt.

Research projects across the world have discovered strong patterns linking highly lucid venerable people. These include above-average education, acceptance of change, satisfying personal accomplishments, physical exercise, a clever spouse, and a strong engagement with life, including reading, social activity, travel, keeping up with new ideas, and regularly solving puzzles.

Not all the things we assume to be engagement are actually helpful, however. Useful intellectual pursuits are the actively stimulating ones – such as solving jigsaws, crosswords and other puzzles, playing chess, and reading books that stimulate the imagination or require some mental effort to properly digest. However, passive intellectual pursuits may actually hasten the mind's decay. Watching television is the most damaging such pastime, but surprisingly anything that makes you "switch off" mentally can also be harmful, such as listening to certain types of music, reading very low-content magazines and even getting most of your social exposure on the telephone. For social interaction to be helpful, it may really need to be face to face.

The Columbia study

A team of researchers from Columbia University in New York tracked more than 1,750 pensioners from the northern Manhattan region over a period of seven years. The subjects underwent periodic medical and psychological examination to assess both their mental health and the physical condition of their brains. Participants also provided the researchers with detailed information regarding their daily activities. The study found that even when you remove education and career attainment from the equation, leisure activity significantly reduced the risk of dementia.

The study's author, Dr Yaakov Stern, found that "Even when controlling for factors like ethnic group, education and occupation, subjects with high leisure activity had 38% less risk of developing dementia." Activities were broken into three categories: physical, social and intellectual. Each one was found to be beneficial, but the greatest protection came from intellectual pursuits. The more activity, the greater the protection – the cumulative benefit of each separate leisure pursuit was found to be 8%. Stern also found that leisure activity helped to prevent the physical damage caused by Alzheimer's from actually manifesting as dementia:

"Our study suggests that aspects of life experience supply a set of skills or repertoires that allow an individual to cope with progressing Alzheimer's Disease pathology for a longer time before the disease becomes clinically apparent. Maintaining intellectual and social engagement through participation in everyday activities seems to buffer healthy individuals against cognitive decline in later life."

Staying lucid

There is strong evidence to back Stern's conclusion. Dr David Bennett of the Rush Alzheimer's Disease Center in Chicago led a study that evaluated a group of venerable participants on a yearly basis, and then after death examined their donated brains for signs of Alzheimer's. The participants all led active lives mentally, socially and physically, and none of them suffered from dementia at the time of their death. It was discovered that more than a third of the participants had sufficient brain-tissue damage to warrant diagnosis of Alzheimer's Disease, including serious lesions in the brain tissue. This group had recorded lower scores than other participants in episodic memory tests – remembering story episodes, for example – but performed identically in cognitive function and reasoning tests.

A similar study took place with the aid of the nuns of the Order of the School Sisters of Notre Dame. The Order boasts a long average lifespan – 85 years – and came to the attention of researchers when it became clear that its members did not seem to suffer from any dementia either. The distinguishing key about the Order is that the nuns shun idleness and mental vacuity, taking particular effort to remain mentally active. All sorts of pursuits are encouraged, such as solving puzzles, playing challenging games, writing, holding seminars on current affairs, knitting and engaging with local government. As before, there was plenty of evidence of the physical damage associated with Alzheimer's Disease, but none of the mental damage that usually accompanied it, even in some nonagenarian participants.

Mental repair

Other studies have also tried to enumerate the benefits of mental activity. A massive group study led by Michael Valenzuela from the University of New South Wales' School of Psychiatry tracked data from almost 30,000 people worldwide. The results were clear – as well as indicating the same clear relationship previously found between schooling, career and mental health, people of all backgrounds whose daily lives include a high degree of mental stimulation are 46% less likely to suffer dementia. This holds true even for people who take up mentally challenging activities as they get older – if you use your mind, the brain still adapts to protect it. If you do not use it, the brain lets it falter.

Puzzle solving techniques

Puzzle solving is more of an art than a science. It requires mental flexibility, a little understanding of the underlying principles and possibilities, and sometimes a little intuition. It is often said of crosswords that you have to learn the writer's style to get really good at his or her puzzles, but the same thing applies to most other puzzle types to a certain extent, and that includes the many and various kinds you'll find in this book.

Sequence puzzles

Sequence puzzles challenge you to find a missing value or item, or to complete a pattern according to the correct underlying design. In this type of puzzle, you are provided with enough previous entries in the sequence that the underlying logic can be worked out. Once the sequence is understood, the missing entry can be calculated. When the patterns are simple, the sequence will be readily visible to the naked eye. It is not hard to figure out that the next term in the sequence 1, 2, 4, 8, 16, ? is going to be a further doubling to 32. Numerical sequences are just the expression of a mathematical formula however, and can therefore get almost infinitely complex.

Proper recreational puzzles stay firmly within the bounds of human ability, of course. With the more complex puzzles, the best approach is often to calculate the differences between successive terms in the sequences, and look for patterns in the way that those differences are changing. You should also be aware that in some puzzles, the terms of a sequence may not necessarily represent single items. Different parts or digits of each term may progress according to different calculations. For example, the sequence 921, 642, 383, 164 is actually three simple sequences stuck together - 9, 6, 3, 0; 2, 4, 8, 16; and 1, 2, 3, 4. The next term will be -3325. Alternatively, in puzzles where the sequence terms are given as times, they may actually just represent the times they depict, but they might also be literal numbers, or pairs of numbers to be treated as totally different sequences, or even require conversion from hours:minutes to just minutes before the sequence becomes apparent.

For example, 11:14 in a puzzle might represent the time 11:14, or perhaps the time 23:14 – or the numbers 11 and 14, the numbers 23 and 14, the number 1114, the number 2314, or even the number 674 (11 * 60 minutes, with the remaining 14 minutes also added). As you can see, solving sequence puzzles requires a certain amount of trial and error as you test difference possibilities, as well as a degree of lateral thinking. It would be a very harsh puzzle setter who expected you to guess some sort of sequence out of context however. So in the absence of a clue otherwise, 11:14 would be highly unlikely to represent

11 months and 14 days, or the value 11 in base 14, or even 11 hours and 14 minutes converted to seconds – unless it was given as 11:14:00, of course.

Letter-based sequences are all representational of course, as unlike numbers, letters have no underlying structure save as symbols. Once you deduce what the letters represent, the answer can be obvious. The sequence D, N, O, ? may seem abstract, until you think of months of the year in reverse order. In visual sequences – such as pattern grids – the sequence will always be there for you to see, and your task is to look for repeating patterns. As with number sequences, easy grids can be immediately apparent. In harder puzzles, the sequences can become significantly long, and often be presented in ways that make them difficult to identify. Puzzle setters love to start grids of this type from the bottom right-hand square, and then progress in spirals or in a back-and-forth pattern – sometimes even diagonally.

Odd-one-out problems are a specialised case of sequence pattern where you are given the elements of a sequence or related set, along with one item that breaks the sequence. Like other sequence puzzles, these can range from very easy to the near-impossible. Spotting the odd one in 2, 4, 6, 7, 8 is trivial. It would be almost impossible to guess the odd item from the set of B, F, H, N, O unless you already knew that the set in question was the physical elements on the second row of the standard periodic table. Even then, you might need a copy of the periodic table itself to notice that hydrogen, H, is on the first row. As with any other sequence problem, any odd-one-out should contain enough information in the puzzle, accompanying text and title to set the context for finding the correct answer. In the above case, a puzzle title along the lines of "An Elementary Puzzle" would probably be sufficient to make it fair game.

Equation puzzles

Equation puzzles are similar to sequences, but require a slightly different methodology. In these problems, you are given a set of mathematical calculations that contain one or more unknown terms. These may be represented as equations, as in the traditional form of $2x + 3y = 9$, or they may be presented visually, for example as two anvils and three iron bars on one side of a scale and nine horseshoes balancing on the other side of the scale. For each unknown – x, y, anvils, etc – you need one equation or other set of values before you can calculate a definitive answer. If these are lacking, you cannot get the problem down to just one possible solution. Take the equation above, $2x + 3y = 9$. There are two unknowns, and therefore many answers. For example, x can be 3 and y can be 1 – for x, $2 * 3 = 6$; for y, $3 * 1 = 3$, and overall, $6 + 3 = 9$ – but x can also be 1.5 and y can be 2… and an infinite range of other possibilities. So when solving equation puzzles, you need to consider all the equations together before you can solve the problem.

To return to our example equation above, if you also knew that $x + 2y = 7$, you could then begin to solve the puzzle. The key with equation problems is to get your equation down to containing just one unknown term, which then lets you get a value for that term, and in turn lets you get the value of the other unknown/s. So, for example, in our previous equations

(2x + 3y = 9 and x + 2y = 7) you could manipulate one equation to work out what x actually represents in terms of y ("How many y is each x?") in one equation, and then replace the x in the other equation with its value in y, to get a calculation that just has y as the sole unknown factor. It's not as confusing as it sounds so long as you take it step by step:

We know that

x + 2y = 7

Any change made to both sides of an equation balances out, and so doesn't change the truth of the equation. For example, consider 2 + 2 = 4. If you add 1 to each side, the equation is still true. That is, 2 + 2 + 1 = 4 + 1. We can use this cancelling out to get x and y on opposite sides of the equation, which will let us represent x in terms of y:

x + 2y - 2y = 7 - 2y.

Now the + 2y - 2y cancels out:

x = 7 - 2y.

Now we know x is a way of saying "7 - 2y", we can replace it in the other equation. 2x + 3y = 9 becomes:

2 * (7 - 2y) + 3y = 9.

Note 2x means that x is in the equation twice, so our way of re-writing x as y needs to be doubled to stay accurate. Expanding that out:

**(2 * 7) - (2 * 2y) + 3y = 9, or
14 - 4y + 3y = 9.**

The next step is to get just amounts of y on one side, and numbers on the other.

14 - 4y + 3y - 14 = 9 - 14.

In other words,

-4y + 3y = -5.

Now, -4 + 3 is -1, so:

-y = -5, and that means y = 5.

Now you can go back to the first equation, x + 2y = 7, and replace y to find x.

**x + (2 * 5) = 7
x + 10 = 7
x + 10 - 10 = 7 - 10
x = 7 - 10**

and, finally.

x = -3.

As a last step, test your equations by replacing your number values for x and y in both at the same time, and making sure they balance correctly.

$2x + 3y = 9$ and $x + 2y = 7$.
$(2 * -3) + (3 * 5) = 9$ and $-3 + (2 * 5) = 7$
$(-6 + 15) = 9$; and $(-3 + 10) = 7$.
$9 = 9$ and $7 = 7$.

The answers are correct.

Any equation-based puzzle you're presented with will contain enough information for you to work out the solution. If more than two terms are unknown, the technique is to use one equation to find one unknown as a value of the others, and then replace it in all the other equations. That gives you a new set of equations containing one less unknown term. You then repeat the process of working out an unknown again, until you finally get down to one unknown term and its numerical value. Then you replace the term you now know with its value in the equations for the level above to get the next term, and continue back on up like that. It's like a mathematical version of the old wooden Towers of Hanoi puzzle. As a final tip, remember that you should have one equation per unknown term, and that if one of your unknown variables is missing from an equation, the equation can be said to have 0 of that variable on either or both sides. That is, $4y + 2z = 8$ is the same as $0x + 4y + 2z = 8$.

If you struggle to work out equations just in your mind, then there are two Puzzle Notes pages at the back of the book just for you. Whichever way you work...

Happy puzzling!

EASY PUZZLES

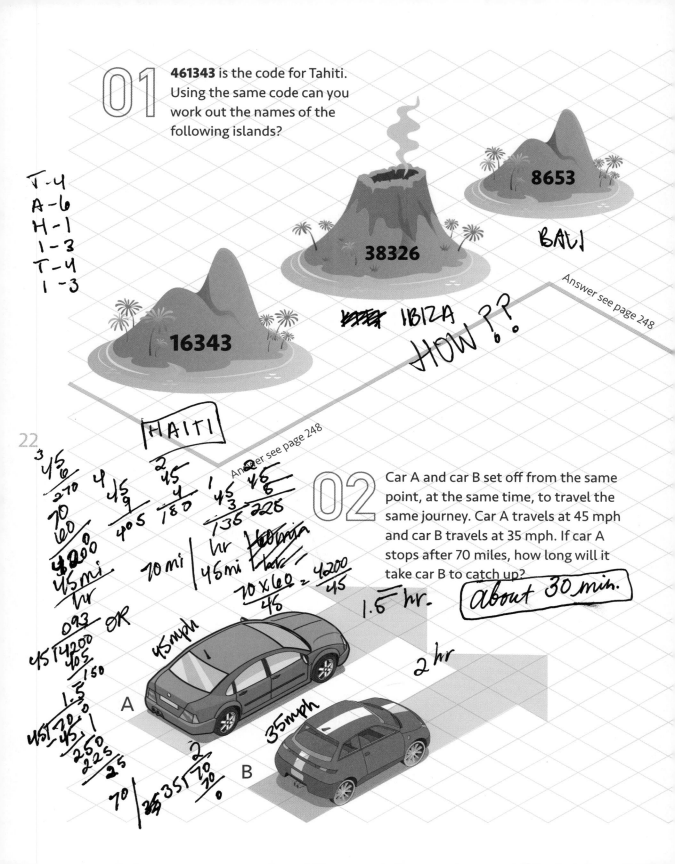

01 461343 is the code for Tahiti. Using the same code can you work out the names of the following islands?

T – 4
A – 6
H – 1
I – 3
T – 4
I – 3

8653

BALI

38326

16343

~~IBIZA~~ IBIZA
HOW ???

HAITI

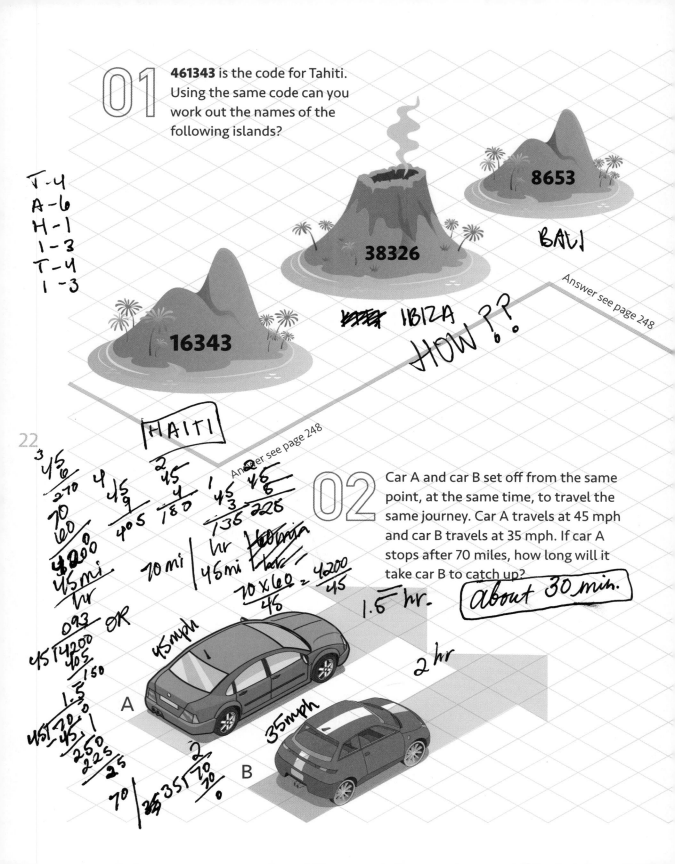

22

Answer see page 248

Answer see page 248

02 Car A and car B set off from the same point, at the same time, to travel the same journey. Car A travels at 45 mph and car B travels at 35 mph. If car A stops after 70 miles, how long will it take car B to catch up?

about 30 min.

1.5 hr.

2 hr

3 4/5/6
270
70
60
4 4/5/9
405
2 45
45/9
4/180
45/3
135
45/6
225
4200
45mi/hr
70mi/hr
45mi/hr
70×60 = 4200/45
093 OR
45)4200
405
150
1.30
45)70.1
-45
250
225
25
70/35 35)70/70/0
A 45mph
B 35mph

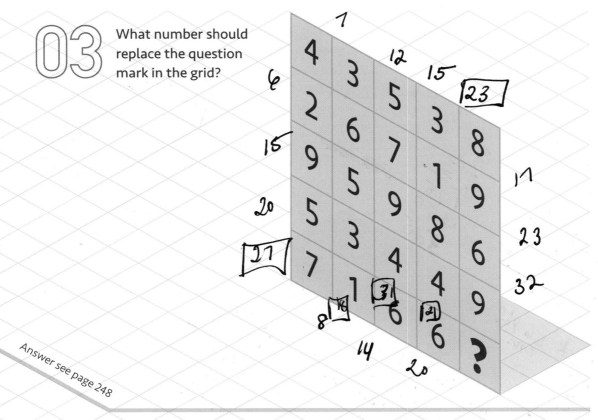

03

What number should replace the question mark in the grid?

Answer see page 248

23

Answer see page 248

04

Assume you are using a basic calculator and apply the mathematical operations <u>strictly in the order chosen.</u> Replace each question mark with a mathematical sign. Plus, minus, multiply and divide can each be used once only. In which order should they be used to score 13?

PEMDAS

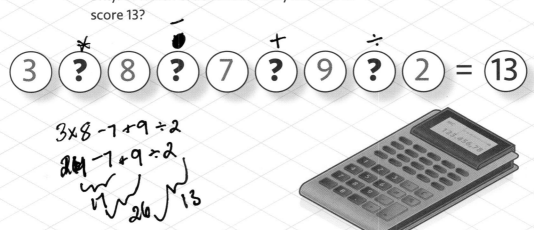

$$3 \times 8 - 7 + 9 \div 2$$
$$24 - 7 + 9 \div 2$$
$$26 \quad 13$$

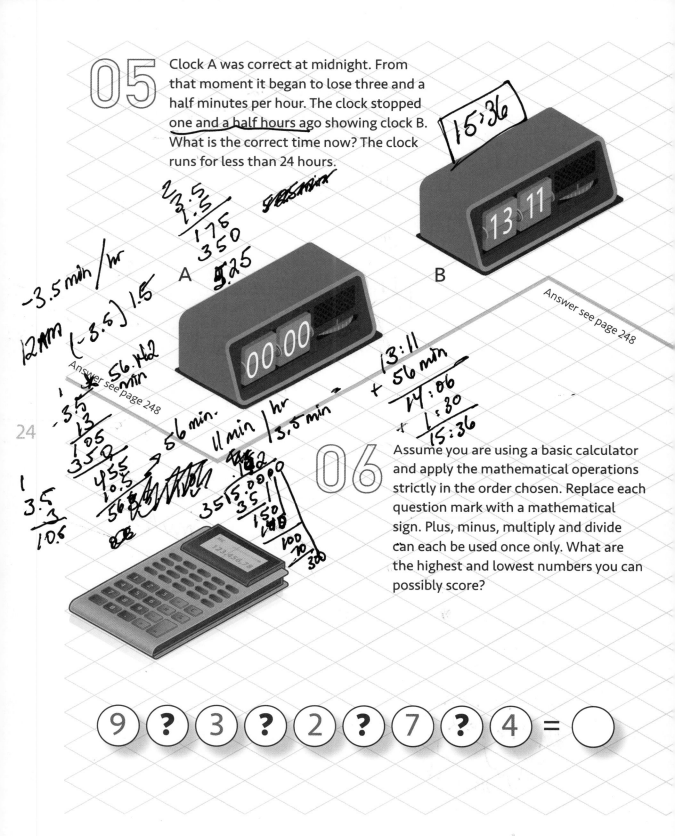

05

Clock A was correct at midnight. From that moment it began to lose three and a half minutes per hour. The clock stopped one and a half hours ago showing clock B. What is the correct time now? The clock runs for less than 24 hours.

A

B

Answer see page 248

Answer see page 248

06

Assume you are using a basic calculator and apply the mathematical operations strictly in the order chosen. Replace each question mark with a mathematical sign. Plus, minus, multiply and divide can each be used once only. What are the highest and lowest numbers you can possibly score?

$$9 \; ? \; 3 \; ? \; 2 \; ? \; 7 \; ? \; 4 = \bigcirc$$

What number should replace the question mark?

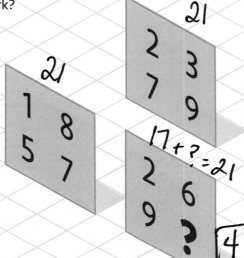

21

2 3
7 9

21

1 8
5 7

21

6 4
3 8

17 + ? = 21

2 6
9 ?

4

Answer see page 248

15   17   19   21   23   25
1 2 3 4 5 6 7 8 9 10 11 12 13 14 16 18 20 22 24 26
A B C D E F G H I J K L M N O P Q R S T U V W X Y Z

15   4

25

Answer see page 248

08 If J Y = 35, CG = 10
and LT = 32, 8
what does BW = ?

21

J + Y = 35
10 + 25 = 35

C + G = 10
3 + 7 = 10

L + T = 32
12 + 20 = 32

B + W = 2 + 23 = 25

*looked at answer before solving

09

A car and a motorcycle set off from the same point to travel the same journey. The car sets off two minutes before the motorcycle. If the car travels at 60 km/h and the motorcycle travels at 80 km/h, how many kilometres from the starting point will they draw level?

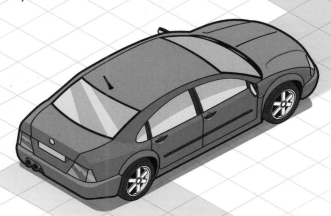

Answer see page 248

10 Clock A was correct at midnight. From that moment it began to lose four minutes per hour. The clock stopped three hours ago showing clock B. What is the correct time now? The clock runs for less than 24 hours.

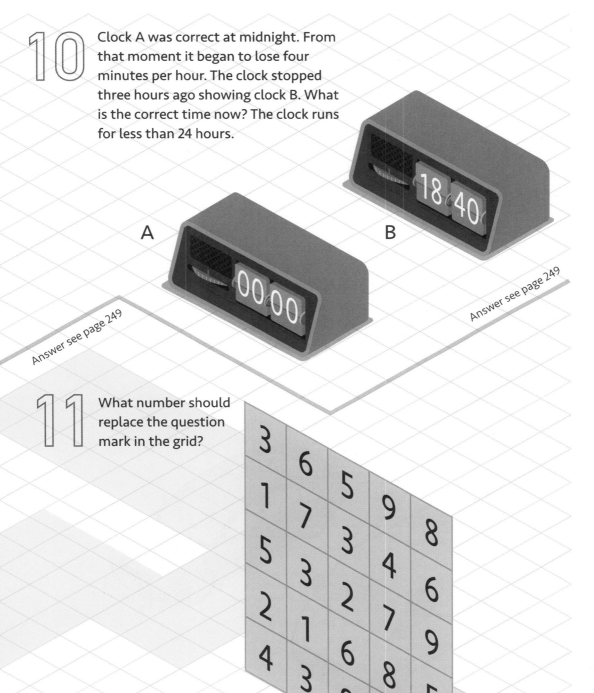

A

B

Answer see page 249

Answer see page 249

11 What number should replace the question mark in the grid?

3	6	5	9	8
1	7	3	9	8
5	3	2	4	6
2	1	6	7	9
4	3	9	8	5
			2	?

12

The alphabet is written here but some letters are missing. Arrange the missing letters to give a word. What is it?

Answer see page 249

B C F G J K L M O
P Q R T U W X Y Z

Answer see page 249

13

Two vehicles set off from the same point to travel the same journey. The first vehicle sets off ten minutes before the second vehicle. If the first vehicle travels at 55 km/h and the second vehicle travels at 60 km/h, how many kilometres from the starting point will the two vehicles draw level?

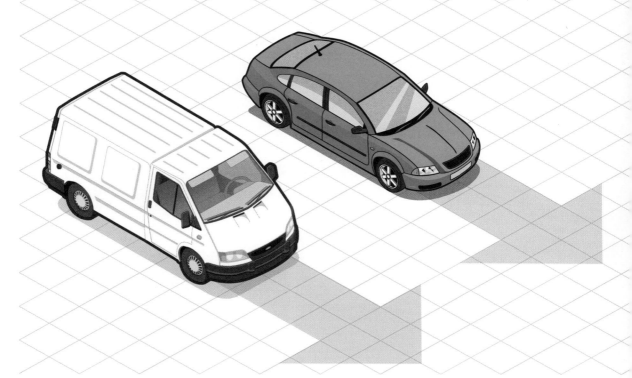

14

If D L = 8, M Z = 13 and A K = 10, what does N R = **?**

Answer see page 249

Answer see page 249

15

What number should replace the question mark?

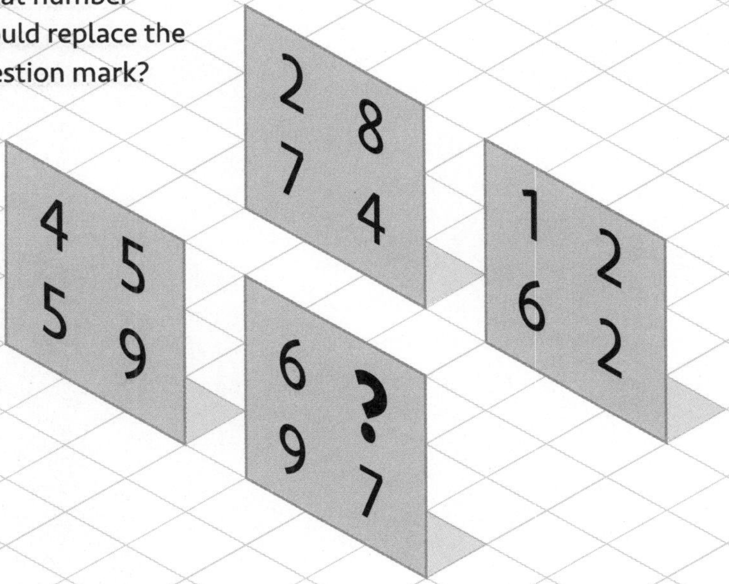

2 8
7 4

4 5
5 9

1 2
6 2

6 **?**
9 7

16 If A+M = 7, E−W = 0
and N−V=1,
what does H+Z = **?**

N − V = 1
E − W = 0
A + M = 7
H + Z = ?

1 2 3 4 5 6 7 8 9 10 11 12 13 14 15 16 17 18 19 20 21 22 23 24 25 26
A B C D E F G H I J K L M N O P Q R S T U V W X Y Z

Answer see page 249

17 Assume you are using a basic calculator and apply the mathematical operations strictly in the order chosen. Replace each question mark with a mathematical sign. Plus, minus, multiply and divide can each be used once only. How many different ways are there to score 5?

Answer see page 249

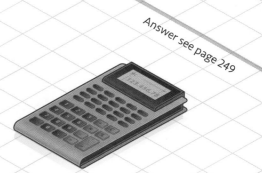

2 ? 3 ? 9 ? 5 ? 8 = 5

18 An airplane covers its outward journey at 555 mph. It returns, over exactly the same distance at 370 mph. What is the airplane's average speed over the entire journey?

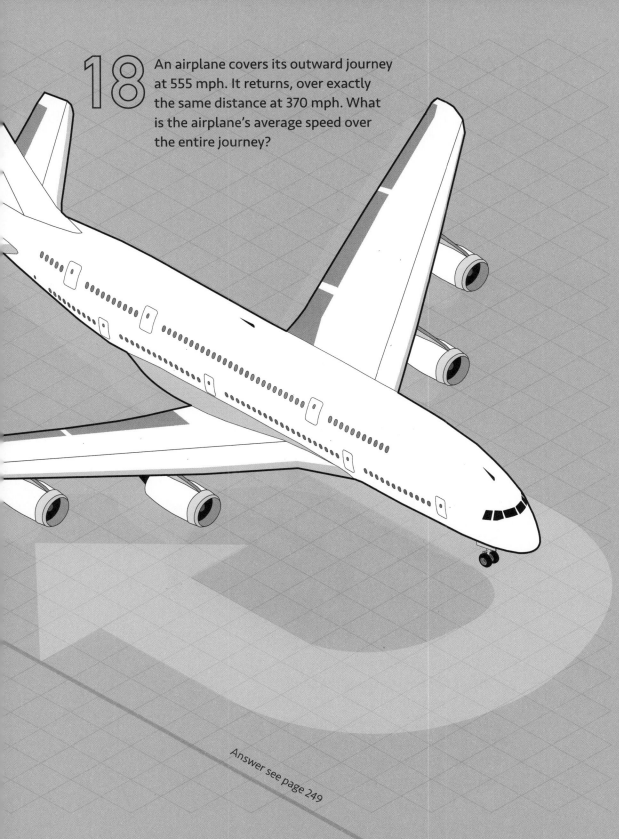

Answer see page 249

19 If CSF = 16, TAQ = 4,
ZOL = 29 and HWM = 18,
what does NER = **?**

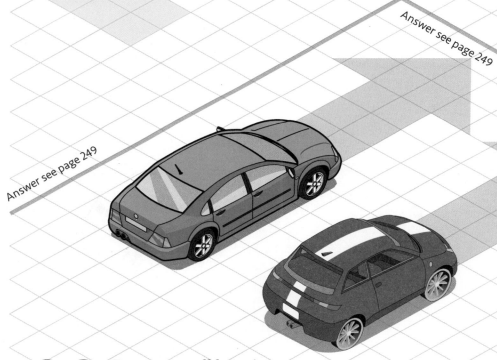

Answer see page 249

Answer see page 249

20 Two cars set off from the same point, at the same time, to travel the same journey. The first car travels at 50 mph and the second car travels at 40 mph. If the first car stops after 90 miles, how many minutes will it take the second car to catch up?

21

A bus has travelled 60 miles at 50 mph. It started its journey with 8 gallons of fuel but its tank has been leaking throughout the journey and is now dry. The bus completes 25 miles per gallon. How many gallons of fuel does it leak per hour?

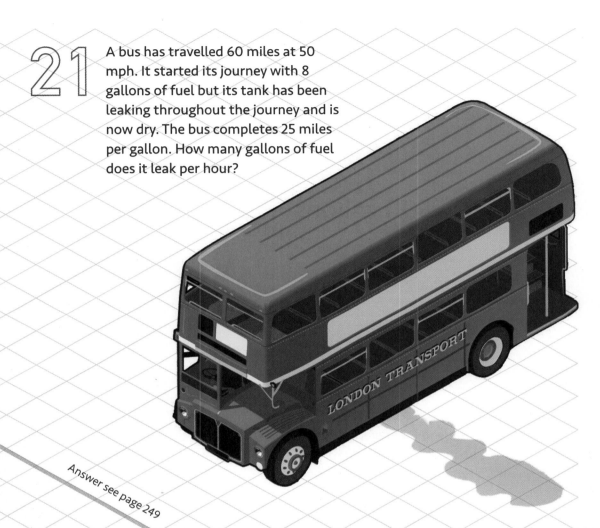

Answer see page 249

Answer see page 250

22

Add together three numbers each time to score 22. Each number can be used as many times as you wish. How many different combinations are there?

2   4   6   8   10   12   14

Answer see page 250

500 gallons

23 A fire engine travels 9 miles to a fire at a speed of 40mph. Its tank holds 500 gallons of water but has been leaking throughout the journey at a rate of 20 gallons per hour. If the fire engine requires 496 gallons of water to extinguish the fire, will it succeed?

24

What number should appear next in this sequence?

3   8   35   48   99   ?

Answer see page 250

Answer see page 250

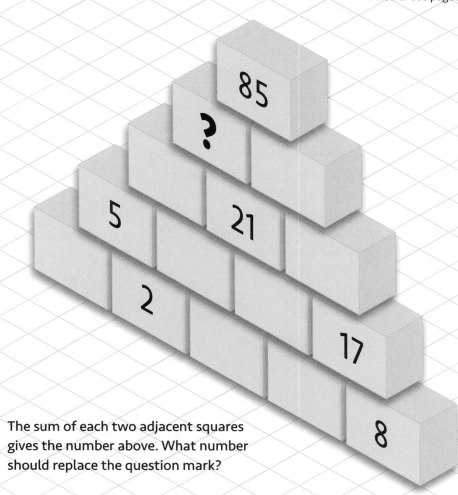

25

The sum of each two adjacent squares gives the number above. What number should replace the question mark?

26

A spaceship covers its journey to Earth at 735 mph. It returns, over exactly the same distance at 980 mph. What is the spaceship's average speed over the entire journey?

Answer see page 250

27

A factory recycles sheets of paper for use in its offices. Six used sheets of paper are needed to make each new sheet. If there are 2331 used sheets of paper, how many new sheets can possibly be made in total?

Answer see page 250

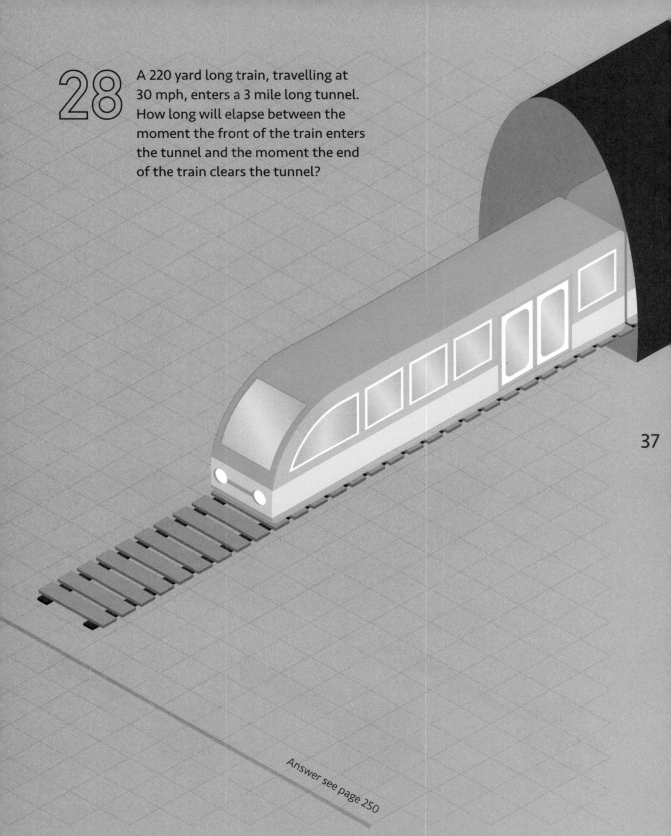

28 A 220 yard long train, travelling at
30 mph, enters a 3 mile long tunnel.
How long will elapse between the
moment the front of the train enters
the tunnel and the moment the end
of the train clears the tunnel?

Answer see page 250

Throw three darts at this board to score 70. How many different combinations are there? Every dart scores.

Answer see page 250

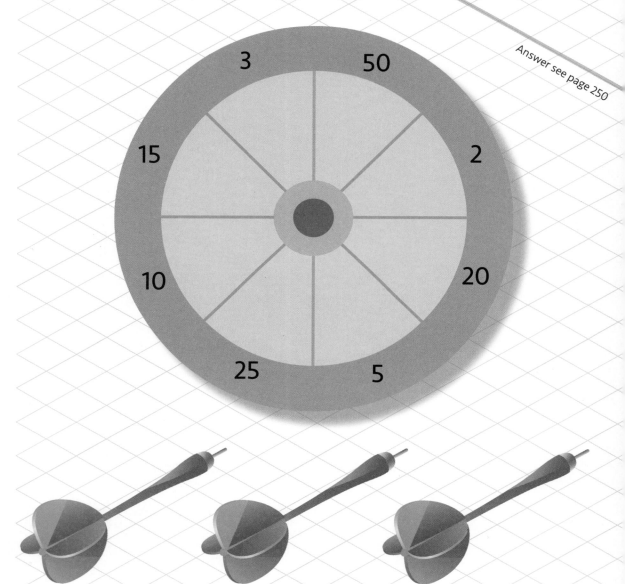

30

A collection raises $20.96. It is made up of four different denominations of coins and the largest denomination is $1. There is exactly the same number of each coin. How many of each coin is there and what are their values? The list of possible coins in the currency is:
1¢, 5¢, 10¢, 25¢, 50¢, $1.

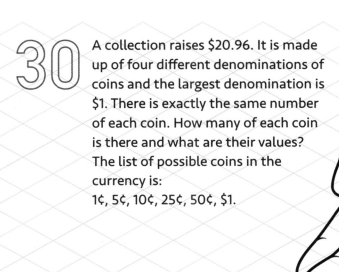

Answer see page 251

31

A car has travelled 40 miles at 30 mph. It started its journey with 10 gallons of fuel but its tank has been leaking throughout the journey and is now dry. The car completes 30 miles per gallon. How many gallons of fuel does it leak per hour?

Answer see page 250

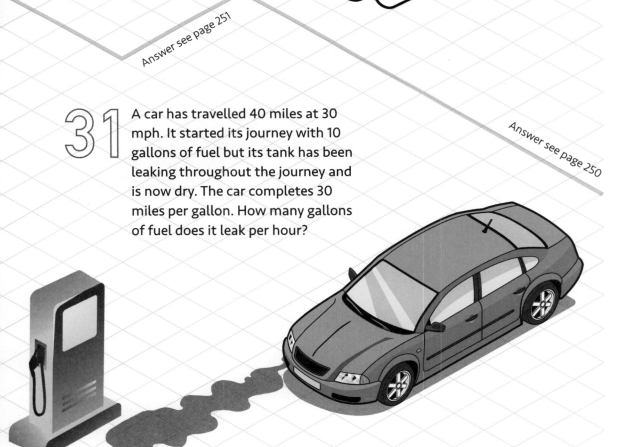

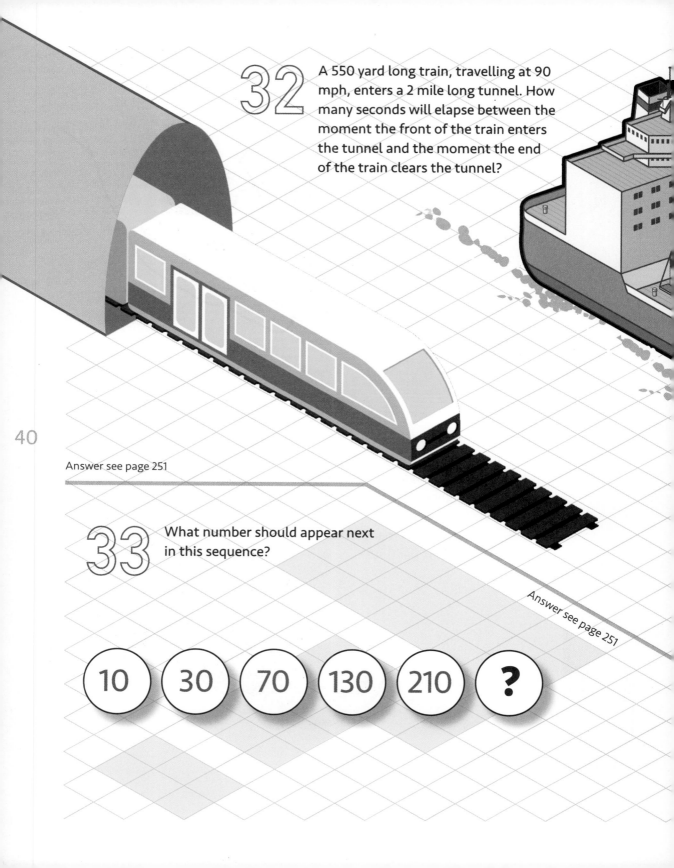

32 A 550 yard long train, travelling at 90 mph, enters a 2 mile long tunnel. How many seconds will elapse between the moment the front of the train enters the tunnel and the moment the end of the train clears the tunnel?

Answer see page 251

33 What number should appear next in this sequence?

Answer see page 251

(10) (30) (70) (130) (210) (?)

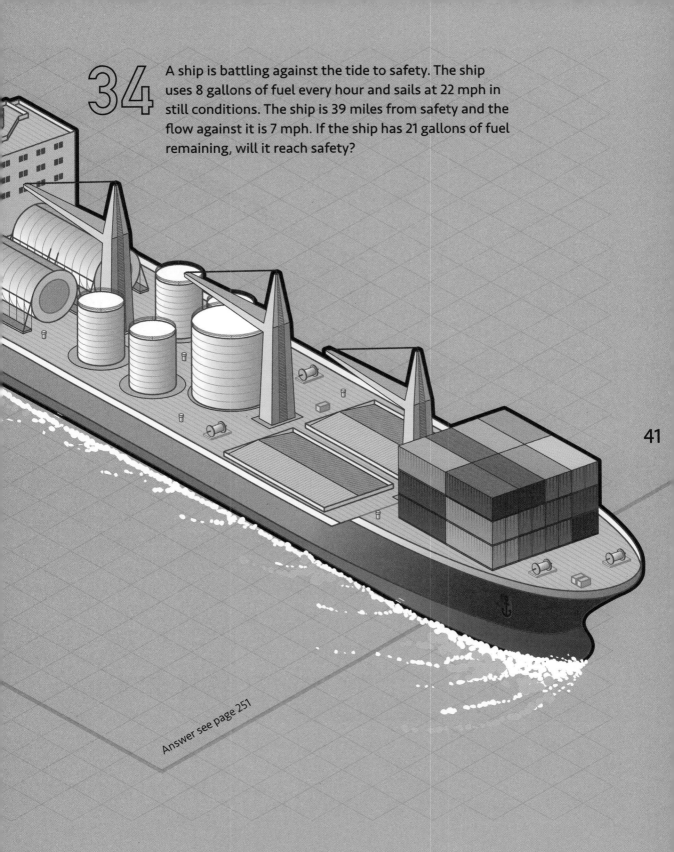

34 A ship is battling against the tide to safety. The ship uses 8 gallons of fuel every hour and sails at 22 mph in still conditions. The ship is 39 miles from safety and the flow against it is 7 mph. If the ship has 21 gallons of fuel remaining, will it reach safety?

Answer see page 251

35 A fire engine travels 7 miles to a fire at a speed of 42mph. Its tank holds 500 gallons of water but has been leaking throughout the journey at a rate of 22.5 gallons per hour. If the fire engine uses 495 gallons of water extinguishing the fire, how much water will it have left over?

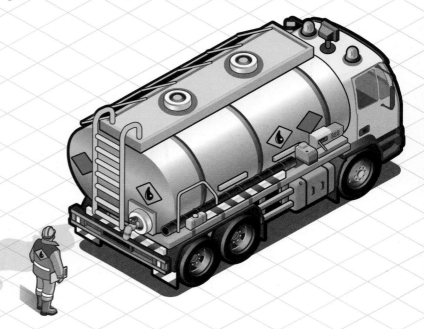

42

Answer see page 251

Answer see page 251

36 What number is missing in this sequence?

5   6   11   17   28   45   ?   118

37 Complete the square with the letters of BEACH so that no row, column or diagonal line of any length contains the same letter more than once. What letter must replace the question mark?

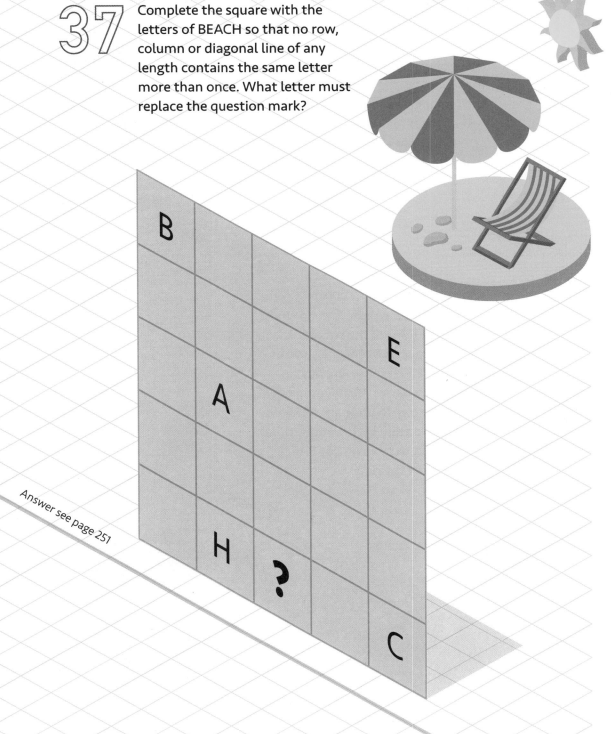

Answer see page 251

38

A group on a five day hiking holiday cover two fifths of the total distance on the first day. The next day they cover one quarter of what is left. The following day they cover two fifths of the remainder and on the fourth day half of the remaining distance. The group now have 15 miles left. How many miles have they walked?

Answer see page 251

Answer see page 251

44

39

A cyclist undertakes a 144-mile cycle ride for charity. On the first day he covers one third of the total distance. The next day he covers one third of what is left. The following day he covers one quarter of the remainder and on the fourth day half of the remaining distance. How many miles will he need to cycle on day 5 to get to the end of the ride?

40

What number should appear next in this sequence?

Answer see page 251

Answer see page 252

41

The sum of each two adjacent squares gives the number above. What number should replace the question mark?

487

?

79   118

55

54

36

42

A factory recycles paper plates for use in its canteen. Nine used plates are needed to make each new plate. If there are 1481 used plates, how many new plates can possibly be made in total?

Answer see page 252

43

What numbers should replace the question marks?

Answer see page 252

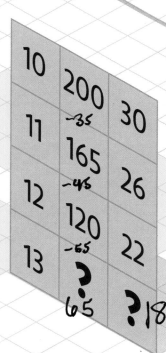

10	200	30
11	-35 165	26
12	-45 120	22
13	-65 ? 65	?18

In which direction should the missing arrow point?

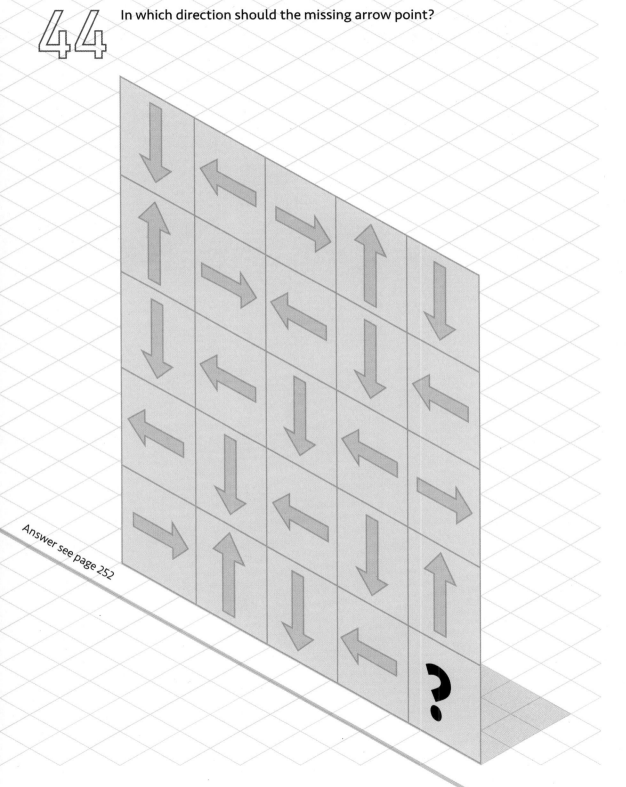

Answer see page 252

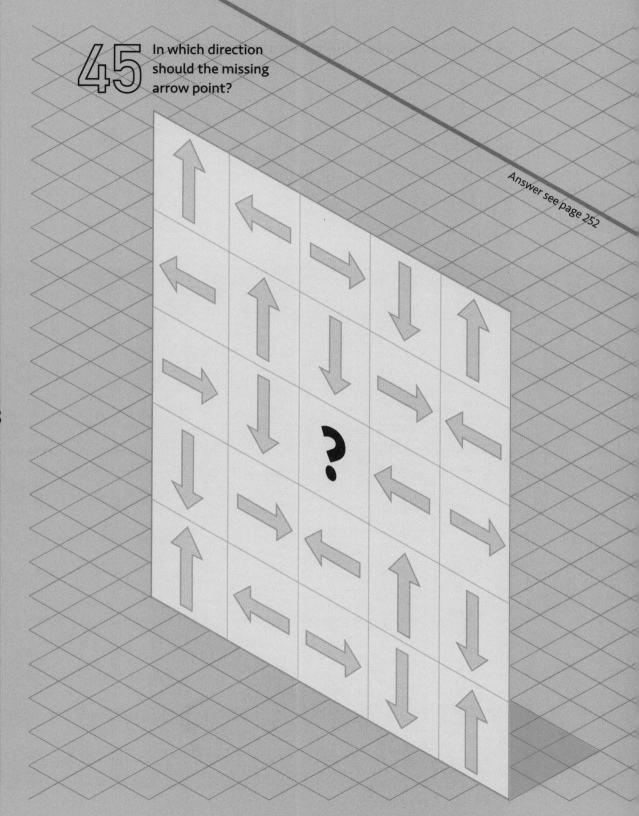

In which direction should the missing arrow point?

Answer see page 252

46 What number should appear next in this sequence?

(1) (20) (300) (3000) (?)

Answer see page 252

Answer see page 252

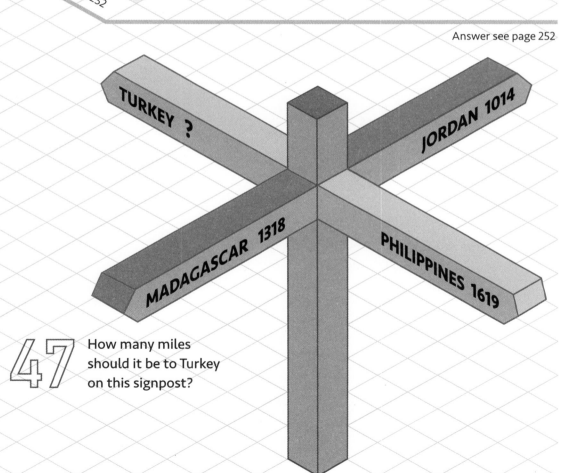

TURKEY ?

JORDAN 1014

MADAGASCAR 1318

PHILIPPINES 1619

47 How many miles should it be to Turkey on this signpost?

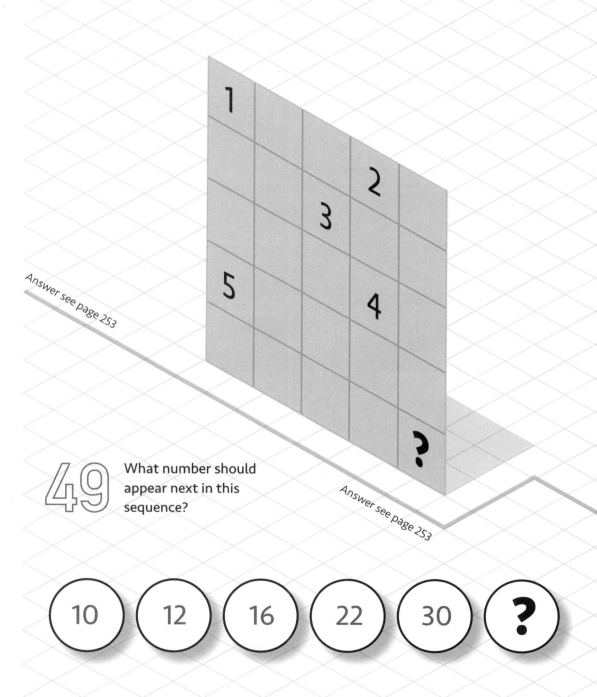

48 Complete the square with the numbers 1 to 5 so that no row, column or diagonal line of any length contains the same number more than once. What number must replace the question mark?

Answer see page 253

49 What number should appear next in this sequence?

Answer see page 253

10　12　16　22　30　?

What is the value of the fourth column?

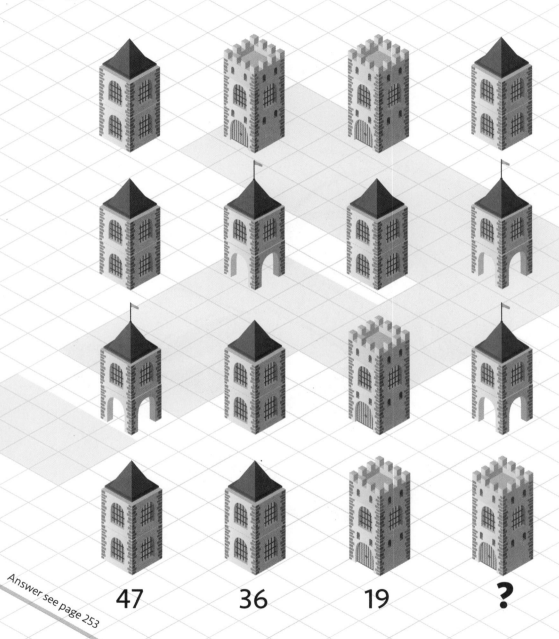

47   36   19   ?

Answer see page 253

51 Car A and car B set off from the same point, at the same time, to travel the same 115 mile journey. If car A travels at 48 mph and car B travels at 40 mph, what will be the difference in their arrival times?

A

B

Answer see page 253

52 What number should replace the question mark?

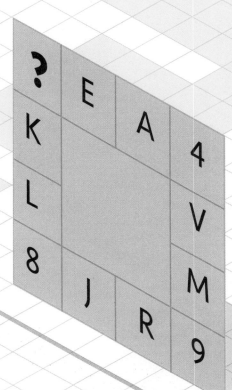

Answer see page 253

53 What letter should replace the question mark?

Answer see page 253

DLH   PUE   BTR   KYN   MWJ   E ? A

Answer see page 253

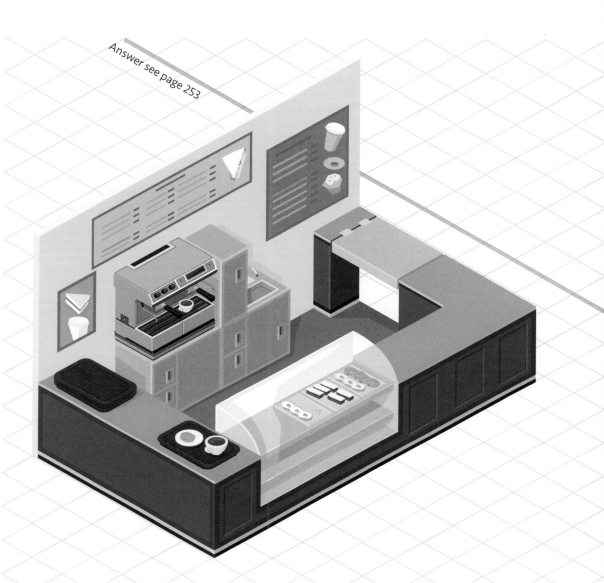

54

54 There are seven items on a deli counter. The pastries are between the pickles and the curries. The salads are next to the samosas. There are two items between the ham and the curries and the ham is between the pickles and the cheese. The pastries are in the exact centre and the salads are at the far end of the counter.

What is the order of the seven items?

55 The sum of each two adjacent squares gives the number above. What number should replace the question mark?

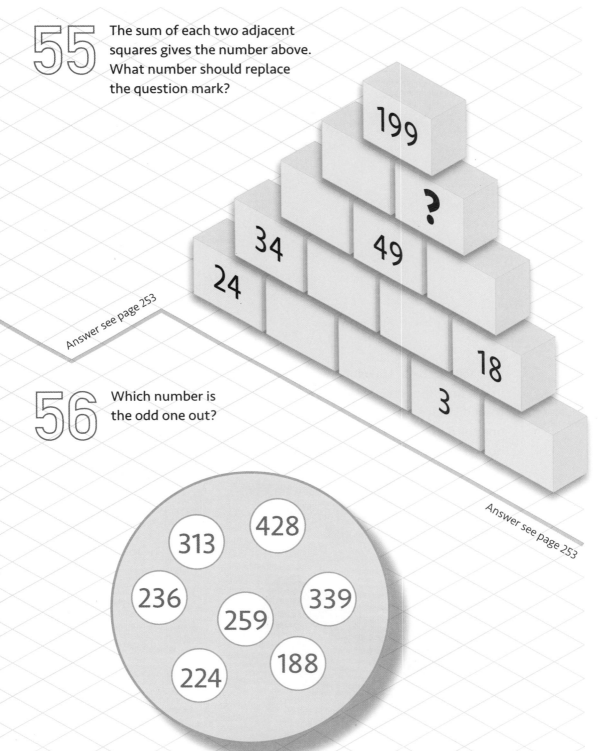

199

?

34   49

24

18

3

Answer see page 253

56 Which number is the odd one out?

313   428

236   339

259

224   188

Answer see page 253

57 What number is missing in this sequence?

(2) (12) (30) (56) (?) (132)

Answer see page 253

58
A coach has been travelling for four hours. In the first hour it covered one third of the total distance. The next hour it covered one third of what was left. The following hour it covered one quarter of the remainder and in the fourth hour half of the remaining distance. The coach now has 25 miles left to its destination. How many miles has it travelled?

Answer see page 253

59

In which direction should the missing arrow point?

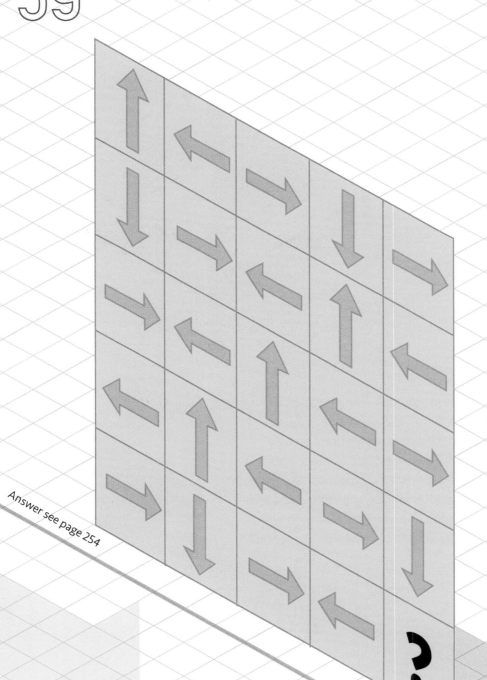

Answer see page 254

60

A factory recycles cups for use in its canteen. Eight used cups are needed to make each new cup. If there are 736 used cups, how many new cups can possibly be made in total?

Answer see page 254

Answer see page 254

61

Assume you are using a basic calculator and apply the mathematical operations strictly in the order chosen. Replace each question mark with a mathematical sign. Plus, minus, multiply and divide can each be used once only. In which order should they be used to score 3?

(4) (?) (5) (?) (9) (?) (8) (?) (7) = (3)

62 What number should replace the question mark?

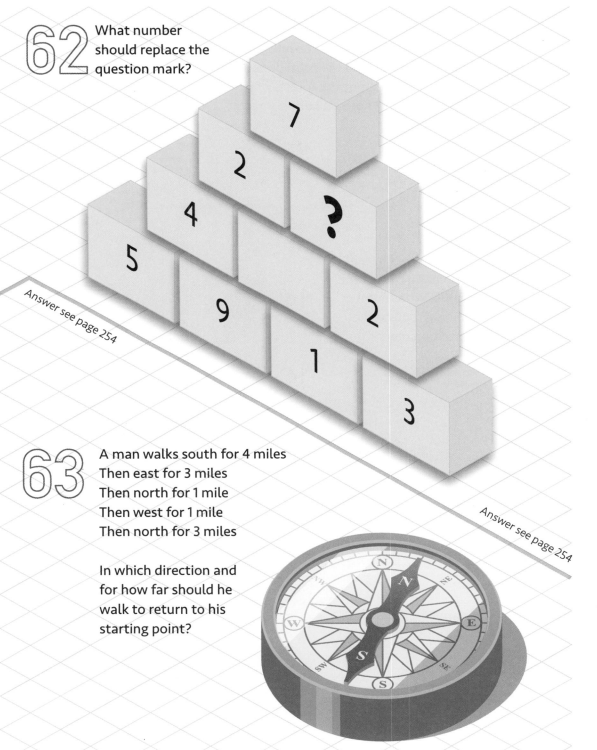

7

2

4   ?

5   2

9

1

3

Answer see page 254

63 A man walks south for 4 miles
Then east for 3 miles
Then north for 1 mile
Then west for 1 mile
Then north for 3 miles

In which direction and for how far should he walk to return to his starting point?

Answer see page 254

64 If Andrew likes the riverbank but not the shore, Michael likes the hills but not the valleys, and Malcolm likes the countryside but not the forest, which location does Thomas like?

A. The plains
B. The meadow
C. The taiga
D. The badlands
E. The tundra

Answer see page 254

Answer see page 254

65 Each symbol in the grid has a consistent value. What number should replace the question mark?

49
44
49
44

44
44
?
35

66 When the following grid is completed correctly, it will contain six different numbers that can follow 651 to produce a six-digit number that has 163 as a divisor.

Answer see page 254

6	5	1

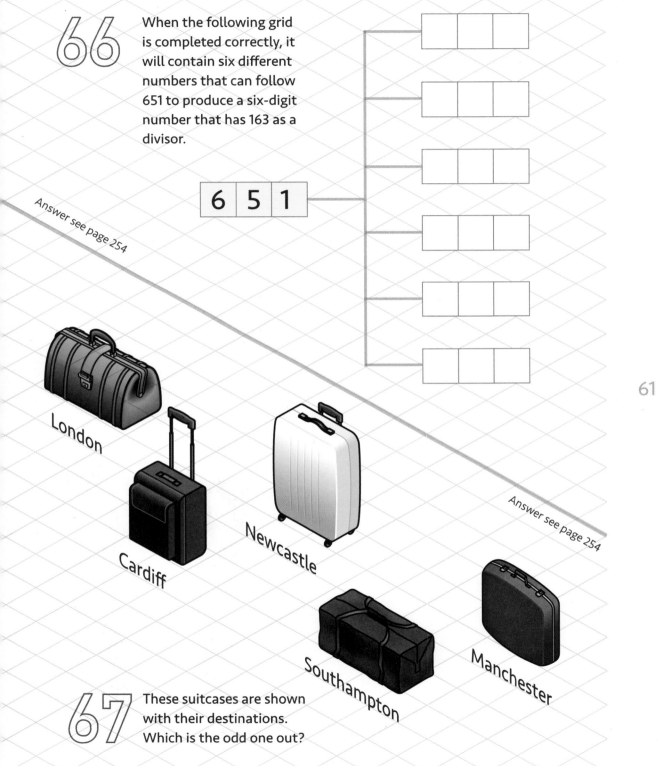

London

Cardiff

Newcastle

Southampton

Manchester

Answer see page 254

67 These suitcases are shown with their destinations. Which is the odd one out?

68

Several famous musical albums have been encoded using the key below. Can you decipher them?

1	2	3	4	5	6	7	8	9
a	b	c	d	e	f	g	h	i
j	k	l	m	n	o	p	q	r
s	t	u	v	w	x	y	z	

2	5	5	9	7	5	5	1	9	1	1	2	3	9	4	1	7	9	5	9	7	8	2	9	6	5	4	5	9
5	8	9	2	5	5	7	9	8	6	3	1	2	6	5	9	2	8	5	9	2	6	4	7	7	3	1	9	4
7	9	5	2	9	6	3	6	7	4	9	2	8	5	9	4	1	9	2	9	1	9	4	5	9	6	6	9	2	8	5	9	4	6	6	5
3	5	3	9	5	5	5	9	4	9	6	5	9	6	1	3	3	9	5	7	9	9	5	2	6	9	7	6	3

Answer see page 254

Answer see page 254

69

A group of one hundred people is made up of individuals who are either corrupt or honest. At least one of them is honest, but from any pair, at least one is corrupt.

How many of each are there?

70 Can you find the square which contains the number in this grid that is 3 squares from itself plus fifteen, 2 squares from itself minus twelve, 6 squares from itself plus five, and 7 squares from itself minus four? All distances are in straight orthogonal lines.

	A	B	C	D	E	F	G	H	I
1	52	9	35	11	18	16	80	7	21
2	29	15	70	89	75	9	78	86	4
3	58	26	4	6	70	52	15	72	84
4	17	37	85	54	53	87	38	97	8
5	72	21	92	83	38	2	39	56	84
6	43	61	25	96	33	19	48	39	56
7	54	62	4	47	53	17	49	31	61
8	31	94	29	7	46	11	4	75	88
9	46	8	74	96	83	51	65	36	5

63

Answer see page 255

71

The following tiles have been taken from a five by five square of numbers. When they have been reassembled accurately, the square will show the same five numbers reading both across and down.

Can you rebuild it?

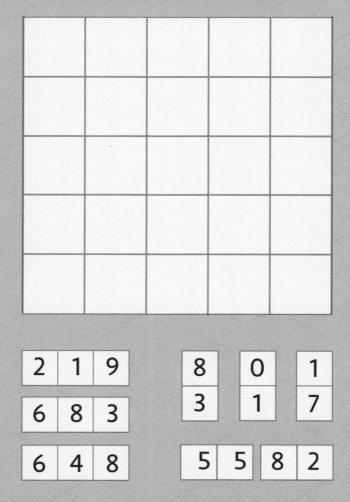

2	1	9

6	8	3

6	4	8

5	1
6	9

8
3

0
1

1
7

5	5	8	2

5	2

Answer see page 255

72

One of the squares in the 3x3 grid is incorrect. Which one?

Answer see page 255

73

Following the logic of this diagram, what symbols should the triangle at the top contain?

Answer see page 255

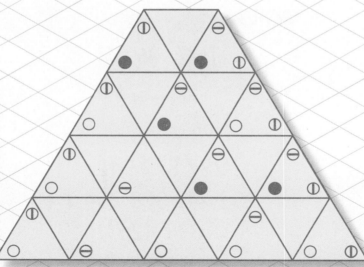

74 The following list of numbers represents places whose letters have been encoded into the numbers needed to reproduce them on a typical phone dial. Can you decode them?

Answer see page 255

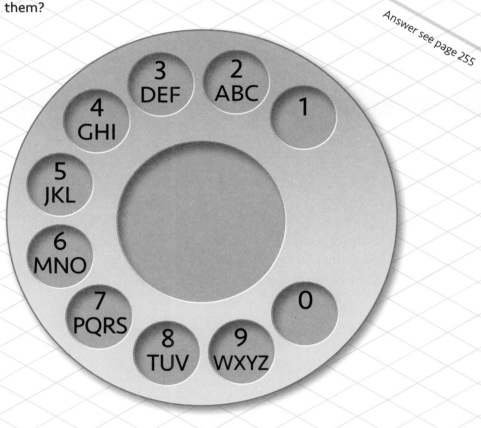

842 632

287 872 542

293 247 378 254 2

639 426

726 852 63

The following diagram obeys a specific logic. What should replace the question mark?

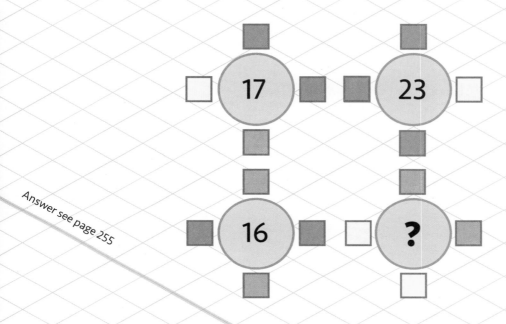

Answer see page 255

76

Using only numbers available in the grid, multiply the smallest triangular number by the largest prime number. What is the result?

Answer see page 255

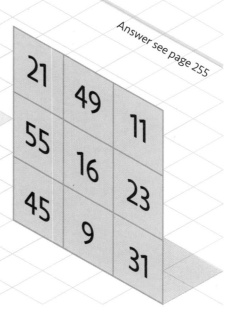

77 There is something wrong with this list. Can you tell what it is?

Bolton

London

Chiang Mai

Paris

Derry

Frankfurt

Cape Town

Rome

Sydney

Madrid

Portland

Athens

Muscat

Prague

Answer see page 255

78 The following terms are all anagrams of chemical elements. Can you disentangle them?

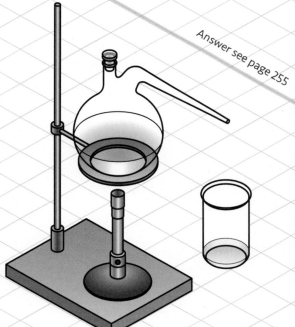

Answer see page 255

AIM SPOUTS

NAG ME SANE

NOBLE DUMMY

HUSH PRO OPS

NERDY HOG

79 Taking a letter from each ball in turn, can you spell out three different world cities?

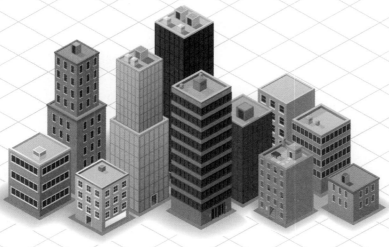

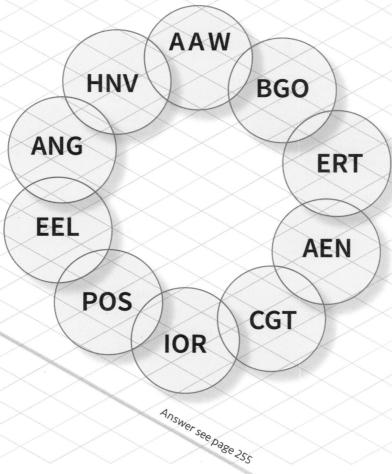

AAW
HNV
BGO
ANG
ERT
EEL
AEN
POS
CGT
IOR

Answer see page 255

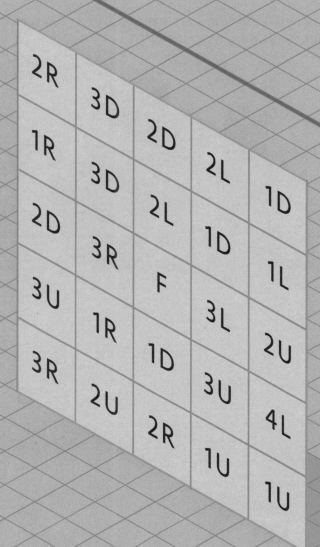

Answer see page 255

The grid contains:

2R	3D	2D	2L	1D
1R	3D	2L	1D	1L
2D	3R	F	3L	2U
3U	1R	1D	3U	4L
3R	2U	2R	1U	1U

80 Each square on this grid shows you the move you must make to arrive at the next square in the sequence, Left, Right, Up, and/or Down. So 3R would be three squares right, and 4UL would be 4 squares diagonally up and left. Your goal is to end up on the finish square, F, having visited every square exactly once. Can you find the starting square?

81 What is the missing letter?

Answer see page 255

82 Can you arrange the following twelve words into four thematically linked groups of three?

Answer see page 256

SNOOK   ABLAITE

PALAIC   SANGUINEOUS

BARBEL   CHAKRAM

GUISARME   RASBORA

UGARITIC   CELADON

AMARANTHINE   FLAMBERGE

This grid obeys a specific sequence. However, some numbers are out of order. When shaded in, these will reveal another number. What is it?

Answer see page 256

72

1	5	3	7	2	6	4	8	0
9	1	7	2	6	4	8	4	8
0	7	1	5	3	7	2	8	4
8	1	9	1	5	3	7	4	6
4	9	0	9	1	5	3	6	2
6	4	8	0	9	1	5	2	7
2	6	4	8	0	9	6	5	3
7	2	6	4	8	4	9	1	5
3	7	2	6	8	8	0	9	1
5	3	7	4	6	4	8	0	9
1	5	0	7	2	6	4	8	0
9	3	5	3	7	2	6	4	8
0	5	1	5	3	7	2	6	4
8	1	9	1	5	3	7	2	6
4	9	0	9	1	5	3	7	2
6	4	9	1	5	3	7	3	7
2	6	4	8	0	9	1	5	3

What is K worth?

$$M + N + N = 39$$
$$K + K + L = 37$$
$$L + M + N = 41$$
$$K + L + N = 36$$

Answer see page 256

Answer see page 256

The following design works according to a certain logic. What number should replace the question mark?

73

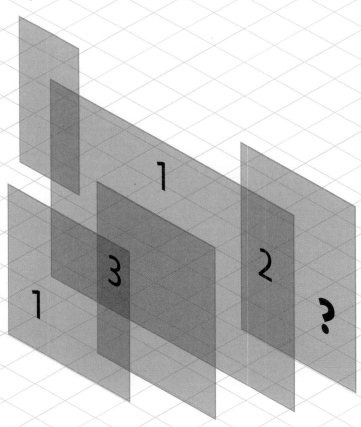

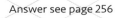

86

What is the missing letter?

A **E** **T** **D**

? **I** **R** **A**

N **U** **G** **L**

Answer see page 256

Answer see page 256

87

The following five items are all districts of a famous city. Can you decrypt them?

CQDXQJJQD

JXU GKUUDI

RHEEABOD

RHEDN

IJQJUD YIBQDT

Can you fill in the numbers provided to correctly complete the grid?

3 digit numbers	5 digit numbers	6 digit numbers	7 digit numbers	9 digit numbers
350	12325	107613	1860589	184399096
637	50435	644059	2818249	327531981
900	57157	744858	3258302	609636074
911	58147	909137	3422047	636969961
	62658		4157622	
	82682		5636795	
	87135		7096359	
	90608		9090680	

Answer see page 256

Can you find your way
through this maze?

Answer see page 256

START

FINISH

I'm literally
so stupid! I
finished I solved
the maze and
didn't realize it g
thought I'd made
a mistake

90

Ten people are collecting their coats after a party, but it is dark, and there is some confusion. Some people may have collected the wrong coat. If nine of the people have the right coat, what is the probability that the tenth has the wrong coat?

Answer see page 256

91

Four 4-letter dog breeds jumbled are in this square. Which pair of letters is not used?

Answer see page 256

LI	CH	PE
SK	PU	OW
SA	YE	TO

92 The letters and numbers in this square obey a certain logic. What number should replace the question mark?

Answer see page 256

78

93 What single letter is missing from each grid?

Answer see page 257

94 This design follows a specific logic.
What should replace the question mark?

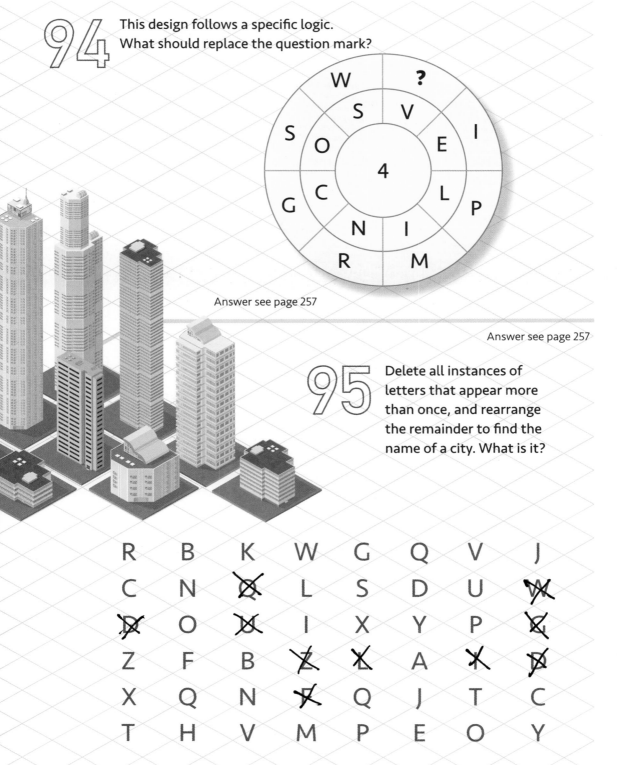

W   ?
S   V
S   I
O   E
4
G   C   L
N   I   P
R   M

Answer see page 257

Answer see page 257

95 Delete all instances of letters that appear more than once, and rearrange the remainder to find the name of a city. What is it?

R	B	K	W	G	Q	V	J
C	N	~~K~~	L	S	D	U	~~W~~
~~D~~	O	~~K~~	I	X	Y	P	~~L~~
Z	F	B	~~J~~	~~L~~	A	~~Y~~	~~D~~
X	Q	N	~~X~~	Q	J	T	C
T	H	V	M	P	E	O	Y

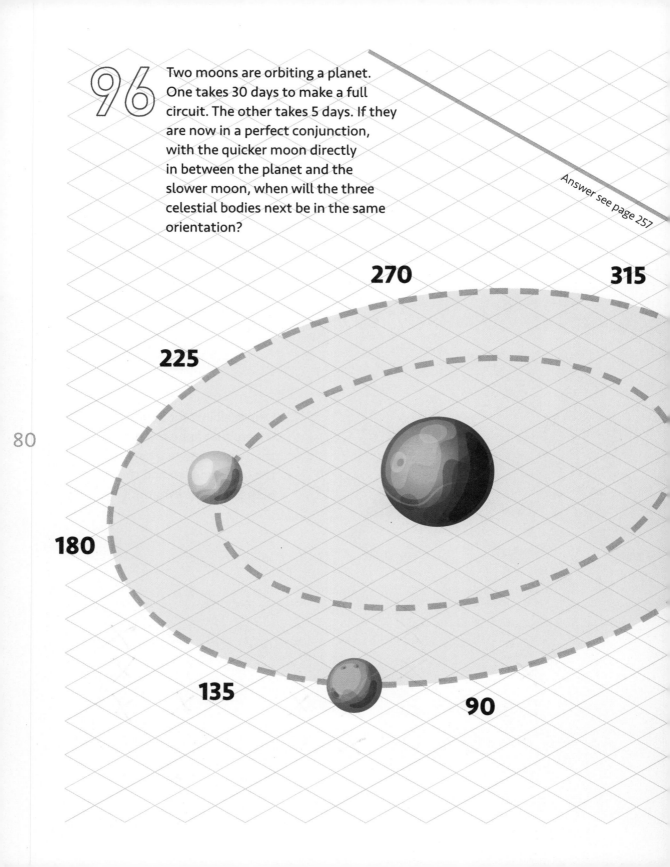

96 Two moons are orbiting a planet. One takes 30 days to make a full circuit. The other takes 5 days. If they are now in a perfect conjunction, with the quicker moon directly in between the planet and the slower moon, when will the three celestial bodies next be in the same orientation?

Answer see page 257

270

315

225

180

135

90

97

In this grid, every row, column and five-figure diagonal adds to 121. The blank spaces each need to be filled by one of four numbers. Can you complete the square?

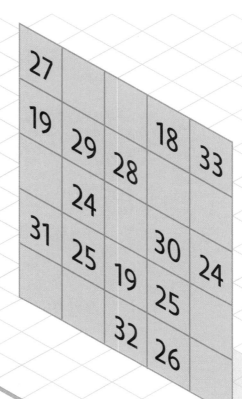

Answer see page 257

0

Answer see page 257

98 Which of these is the odd one out?

A: FORT SUMTER

B: ALAMO

C: FREDRICKSBURG

D: CEDAR CREEK

E: SHILOH

F: FIVE FORKS

G: GETTYSBURG

99 Which of the following numbers is not a numerical anagram of 804,331,088,950,120,324,614?

a. 580,468,043,103,819,201,342

b. 469,018,085,280,303,244,113

c. 400,800,832,192,461,543,831

d. 905,446,102,100,821,833,438

e. 960,330,324,484,180,215,810

f. 433,201,501,314,492,608,880

g. 280,135,248,018,601,039,345

h. 139,541,012,808,624,003,843

i. 280,003,314,468,410,893,152

Answer see page 257

Answer see page 257

100 There is a similarity between the two circles. Knowing that, what number should replace the question mark?

101

Which of the five options A-E below most closely matches the conditions of the top figure?

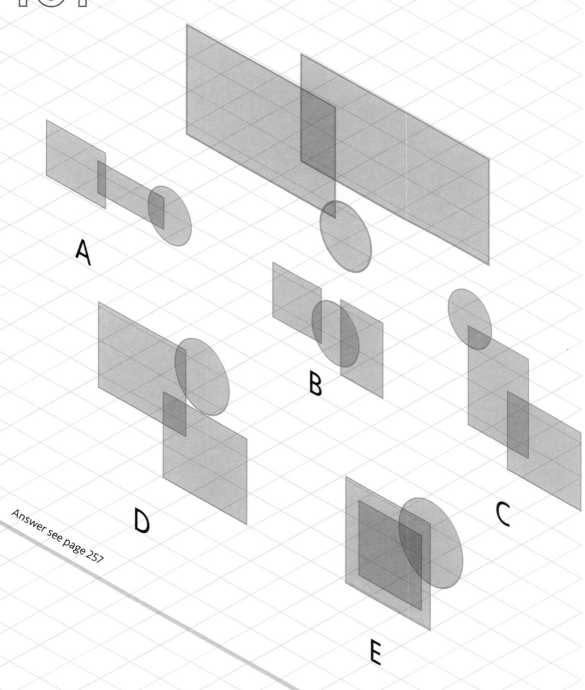

A

B

C

D

E

Answer see page 257

102 Which of these letters does not belong in this triangle?

Z
H
N
G
I
Z
S
A
D
B
W

Answer see page 257

84

103 What should replace the question mark in the final square?

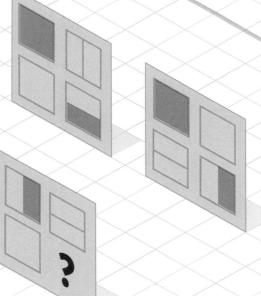

Answer see page 257

The following grid operates according to a specific pattern.
Can you fill in the blank section?

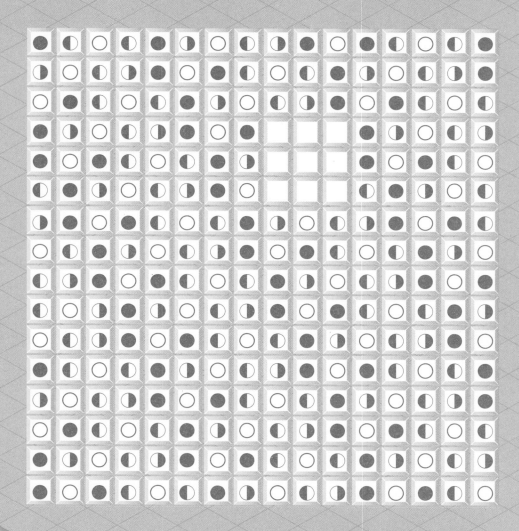

Answer see page 257

105

Which is the odd one out?

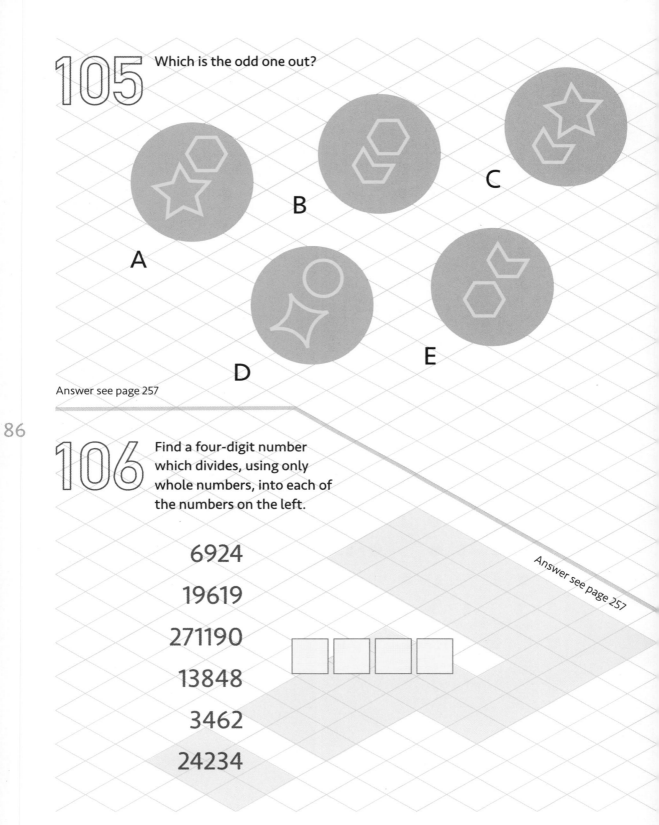

A

B

C

D

E

Answer see page 257

106

Find a four-digit number which divides, using only whole numbers, into each of the numbers on the left.

6924

19619

271190

13848

3462

24234

Answer see page 257

107

Can you find the 36 numbers shown below within the number grid?

1	5	1	2	3	1	2	0	4	5	7	3	7	9	5
9	5	2	4	0	9	9	0	6	9	7	0	2	2	7
1	7	1	2	8	0	2	2	2	4	2	7	1	3	3
9	7	8	5	0	4	5	3	0	4	4	6	7	4	9
4	6	0	0	8	9	9	5	5	5	7	6	3	1	8
8	6	6	7	6	2	6	1	6	1	6	5	2	5	8
5	1	9	8	3	8	1	5	5	8	3	5	1	5	4
3	3	8	0	4	2	1	7	4	4	8	1	1	4	2
5	3	0	9	7	5	5	3	0	7	7	5	0	3	8
3	5	5	0	2	5	5	0	0	8	4	0	9	0	1
1	9	5	1	6	8	5	7	1	3	9	7	3	8	5
1	4	5	9	6	5	3	0	4	7	5	3	0	9	0
6	7	4	3	2	4	4	4	1	1	4	3	7	1	3
2	3	1	8	6	2	2	4	0	1	7	2	7	6	7
3	1	1	9	7	1	6	9	8	5	1	6	7	2	8

256	16728	280222	37495331
433	26113	975530	40172767
676	28150	980345	55508960
1758	45362	1143713	94764403
3349	63874	3186224	99069702
4423	68201	3574035	119716985
5577	110930	5184783	191948535
8379	148491	5576318	204573795
8495	158217	8005520	275125156

Answer see page 258

108

These dominos obey a certain logic. What should replace the question mark?

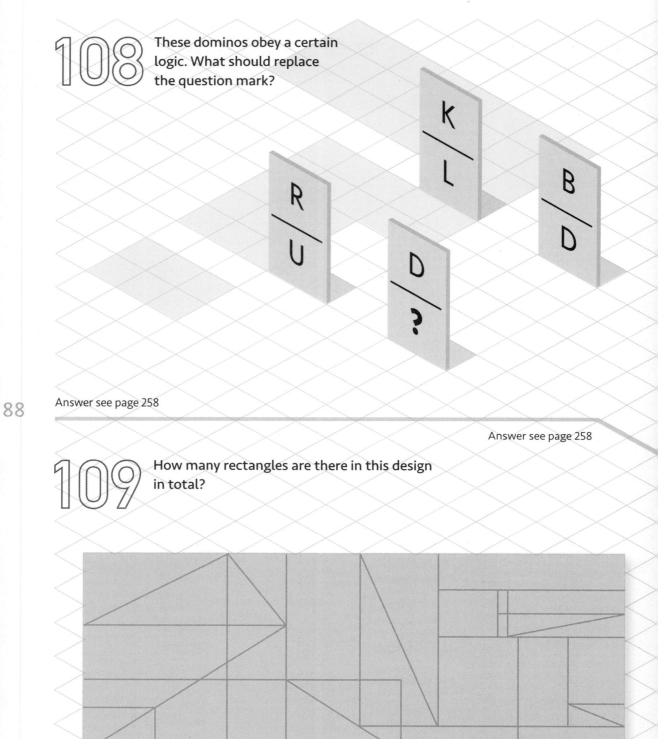

$$\frac{R}{U}$$

$$\frac{K}{L}$$

$$\frac{B}{D}$$

$$\frac{D}{?}$$

Answer see page 258

Answer see page 258

109

How many rectangles are there in this design in total?

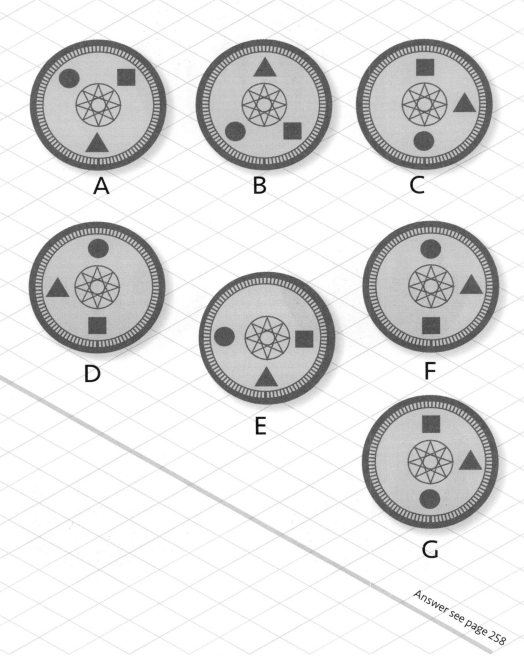

110 Figure A is to figure B as figure C is to which figure?

A

B

C

D

E

F

G

Answer see page 258

111 Which of the shapes below, A-D, fits with the shape above to form a perfect dark circle?

90

A
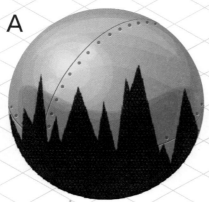

B
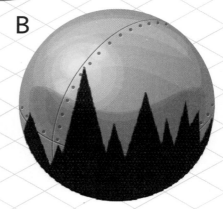

C
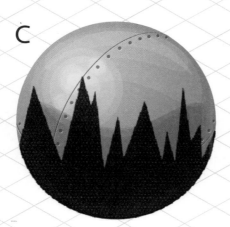

D
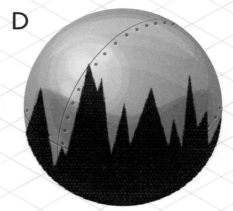

Answer see page 258

112

These numbers, when placed correctly into the grid, will give you two numbers which are multiples of the number 34762. Can you disentangle them?

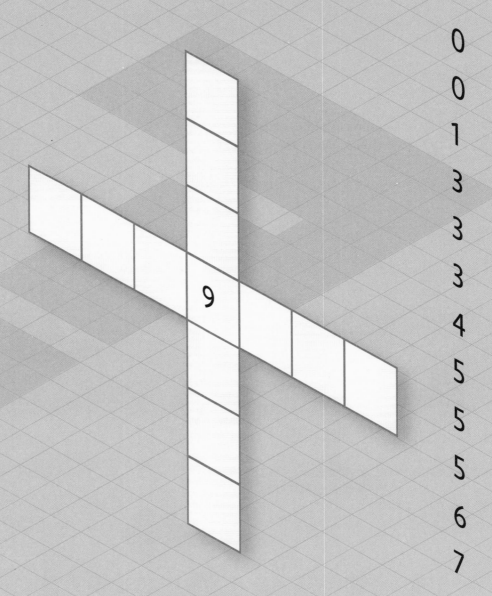

0
0
1
3
3
3
4
5
5
5
6
7

Answer see page 258

113 What are the following nouns all types of?

CRANNOG
GLACIS
CATHAIR
ABATIS
RATH

Answer see page 258

114 Examine the following sets of scales, which are in perfect balance. How many triangles are needed to balance the final scale?

Answer see page 258

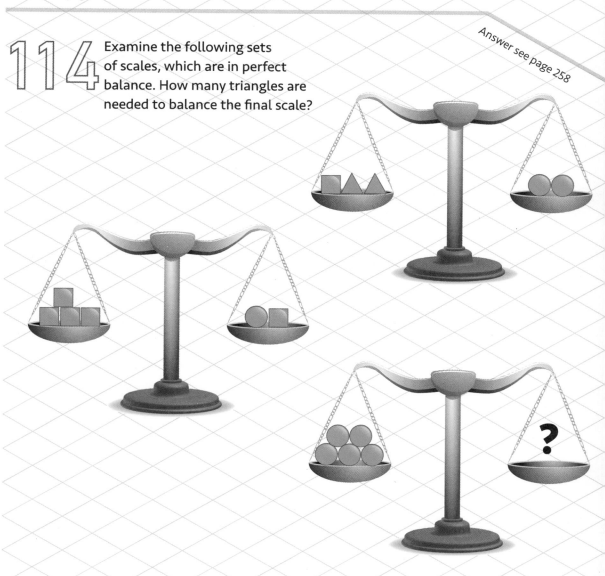

115

Which of the following is not an anagram of a current or former currency?

IRON HIDE   OAK RUN

HARD CAM   PINGS HIP

DIG RULE   ROT MASK

Answer see page 258

Answer see page 258

116

Signs – symbols in a specific position – which appear in the outer circles are transferred to the inner circle as follows: If it appears once or thrice, it is definitely transferred. If it appears twice, it is transferred if no other symbol will be transferred. If it appears four times, it is not transferred.

What does the inner circle look like?

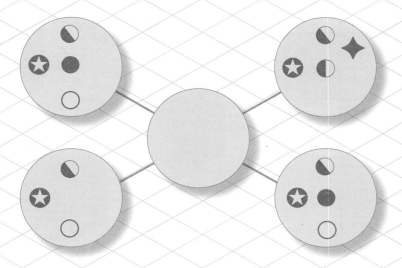

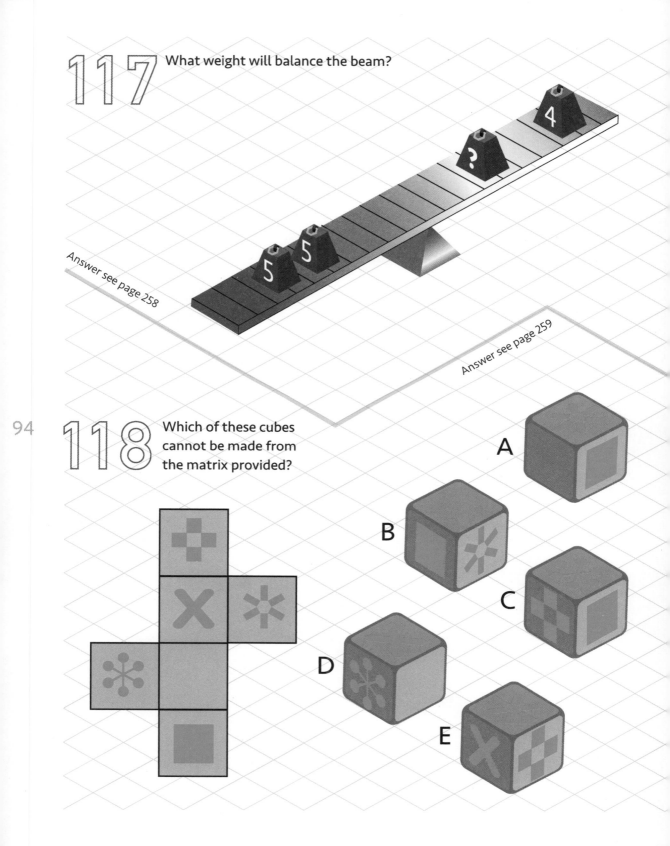

117 What weight will balance the beam?

Answer see page 258

118 Which of these cubes cannot be made from the matrix provided?

Answer see page 259

119

The numbers in this list are sequential terms in a specific sequence of numbers, but they are out of order. What is the sequence?

1220703125
152587890625
1953125
244140625
30517578125
390625
48828125
6103515625
762939453125
9765625

Answer see page 259

120

Find a three-digit number which divides, using only whole numbers, into each of the numbers on the left.

Answer see page 259

35767
3044
362236
14459
6849
120238

121

These rings obey a certain logic. What number should replace the question mark?

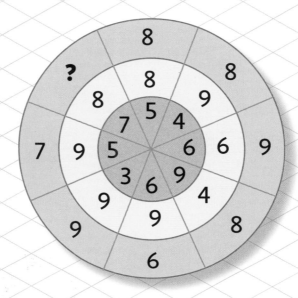

Answer see page 259

Answer see page 259

122

A committee of seven needs to be drawn from twelve people. How many different ways of doing this are there?

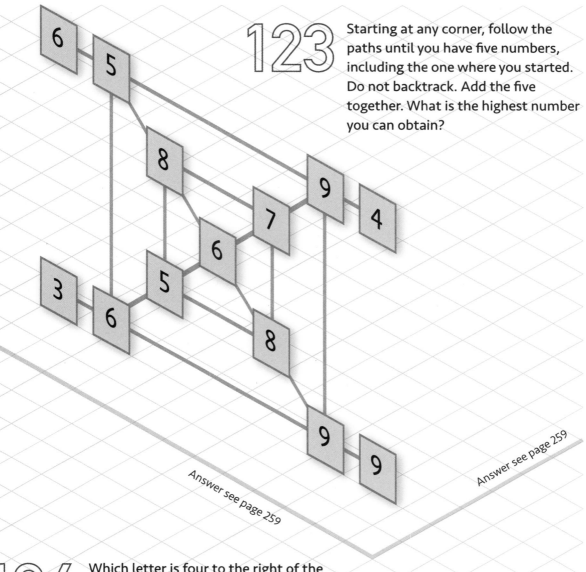

123 Starting at any corner, follow the paths until you have five numbers, including the one where you started. Do not backtrack. Add the five together. What is the highest number you can obtain?

Answer see page 259

Answer see page 259

124 Which letter is four to the right of the letter immediately to the left of the letter four to the left of the letter two to the right of the letter G?

(A) (B) (C) (D) (E) (F) (G) (H) (I) (J) (K) (L)

MEDIUM PUZZLES

What is the value of the fourth column?

100

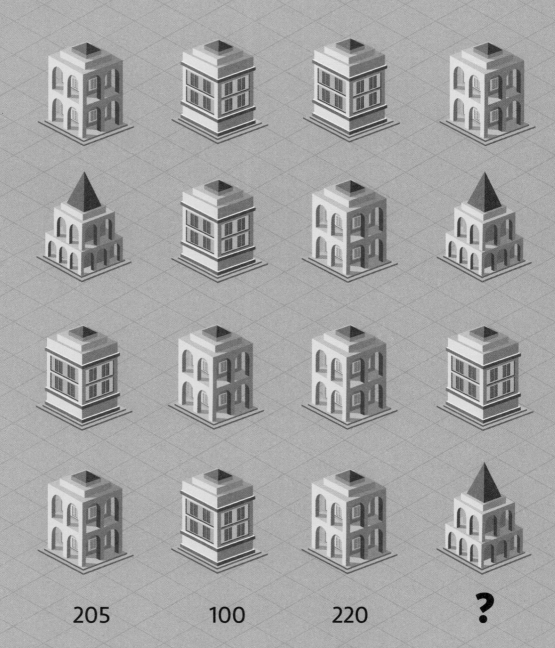

205   100   220   ?

Answer see page 262

02

A ship is battling against a strong tide to safety. It uses eight gallons of fuel every hour and sails at 16 mph in still conditions. The ship is 84 miles from safety and the flow against it is 7 mph. The ship has 75 gallons of fuel left. How much will it have to spare when it reaches the shore?

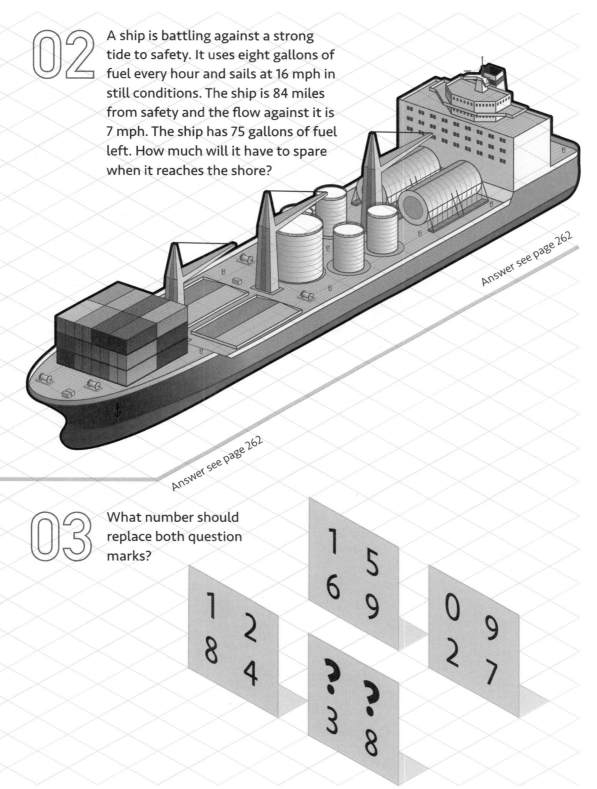

Answer see page 262

Answer see page 262

03

What number should replace both question marks?

1 2
8 4

1 5
6 9

0 9
2 7

? ?
3 8

04 Clock A was correct at midnight. From that moment, it began to lose three and a half minutes per hour. The clock stopped an hour ago, showing clock B. What is the correct time now? The clock runs for less than 24 hours.

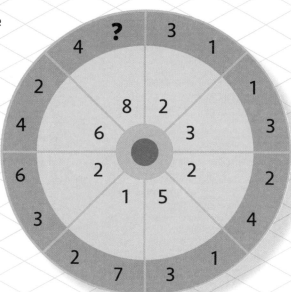

B

A

Answer see page 262

Answer see page 262

05 What number should replace the question mark?

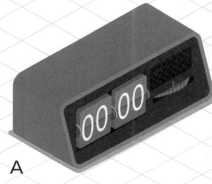

06

What numbers should replace the question marks?

12	4	9
57	19	54
33	11	54
48	11	30
27	16	45
	?	?

Answer see page 262

07

A cyclist rides from one town to another. On the first day he covers one quarter of the total distance. The next day he covers one third of what is left. The following day he covers one quarter of the remainder and on the fourth day half of the remaining distance. The cyclist now has 25 miles left. How many miles has he travelled?

Answer see page 262

08 A 440 yard long tram, travelling at 40 mph, enters a tunnel of one and a half a miles in length. How long will elapse between the moment the front of the tram enters the tunnel and the moment the end of the tram clears the tunnel?

Answer see page 262

09 From a group of office workers, three times as many people choose attending a gym as choose swimming to keep fit. Six more people choose walking than choose swimming and three less people choose jogging than walking. Seven people choose jogging as their favourite activity. How many people choose each of the other activities?

Answer see page 262

10

What should be the value of the fourth row?

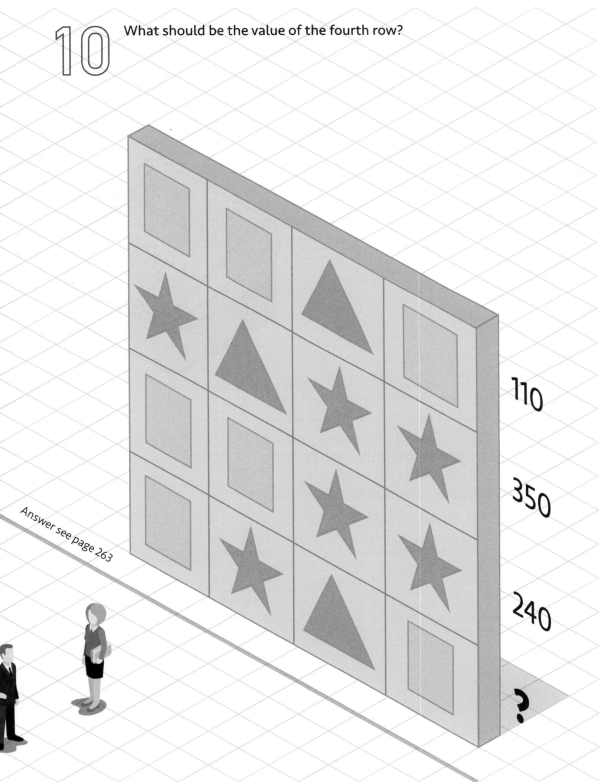

110

350

240

?

Answer see page 263

11

A cash register contains $15.84. It is made up of four different denominations of money and the largest denomination is $1. There is exactly the same number of each denomination. How many of each is there and what are their values?

Answer see page 263

12

A fire engine travels five miles to a fire at 30 mph. Its tank holds 500 gallons of water but has been leaking throughout the journey at a rate of 22.5 gallons per hour. How many gallons of water will the fire engine have available to put out the fire?

Answer see page 263

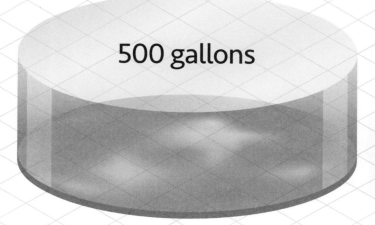

500 gallons

13 Here is an unusual safe. Each of the buttons must be pressed once only in the correct order to reach the centre X and open the safe. The number of moves and direction to move is marked on each button. Which button is the first you must press?

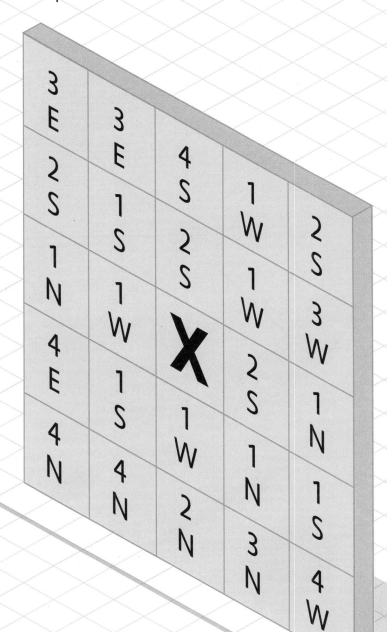

Answer see page 263

14 Throw three darts at this board to score 25. How many different combinations are there? Every dart lands in the board and no dart falls out.

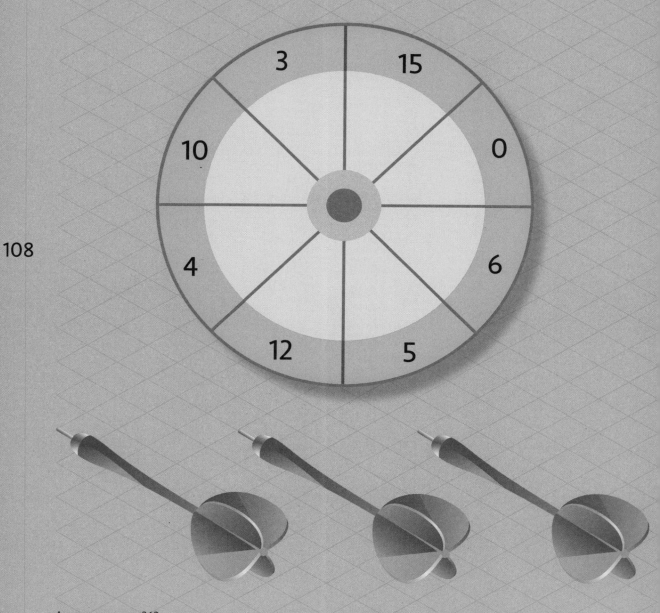

Answer see page 263

15 What is the value of the fourth column?

32   22   21   ?

Answer see page 263

16

What number should replace the question mark?

8   28

12   42

2   7

18   63

10   ?

Answer see page 263

Answer see page 263

17

A car has travelled 30 miles at a speed of 50 mph. It started its journey with 8 gallons of fuel but its tank has been leaking throughout the journey and is now dry. The car completes 25 miles per gallon. How much fuel does it leak per hour?

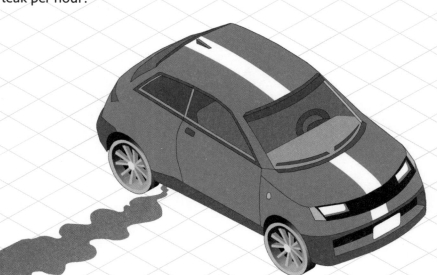

18

In an amateur soccer team's first 15 games, the average number of goals per game was three. After a further 30 games the average goals per game increased to five. What was the average number of goals per game in the last 30 games only?

Answer see page 263

Answer see page 263

19

Add together three numbers each time to score 14. How many different combinations are there? Each number can be used as many times as you wish.

20

A coach and a car set off from the same point to travel the same journey. The coach leaves nine minutes before the car. If the coach travels at 50 km/h and the car travels at 80 km/h, how many kilometres from the starting point will they draw level?

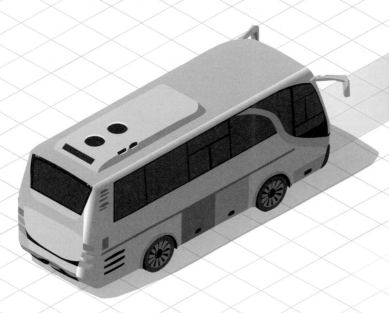

Answer see page 264

Answer see page 264

21

A certain month has five **Sundays** and the first **Saturday** of the month is the 7th.

On what day does the 30th fall?

What will be the date of the third **Monday** of the month?

How many **Fridays** are there in the month?

On what day does the 11th fall?

Answer see page 264

22 What number should replace the question mark in the grid?

5

3

2

1

6

4

8

7

3

2

2

5

5

6

2

4

1

5

9

?

2

2

5

7

1

3

4

23

Using only the numbers and signs given, create a sum where both sides are equal.

6 13 17 25 + ÷ √ = ( )

Answer see page 264

24

Which symbol should replace the question mark to continue the sequence?

#	£	~	%	$
%	$	X	#	£
$	%	#	X	~
£	#	%	~	X
~	X	$	£	?

Answer see page 264

25 A helicopter covers its outward journey at 250 mph. It returns, over exactly the same distance at 166.6666 mph. What is the helicopter's average speed over the entire journey?

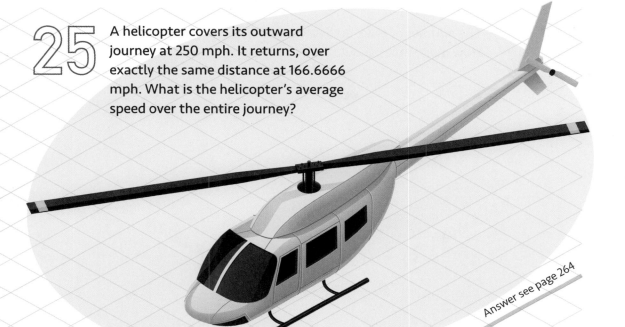

Answer see page 264

115

Answer see page 264

26 284561 is the code for CHAPEL, 67539 is the code for PEACH and 3867 is the code for LEAP.

Which word is 874 in code?

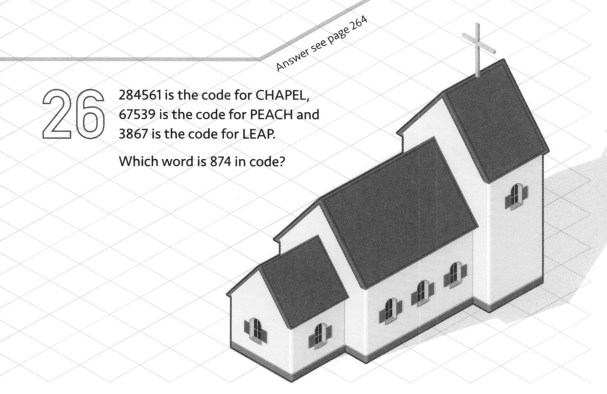

27 The number of miles to deserts is shown on this signpost.
How many miles should it be to the Gobi?

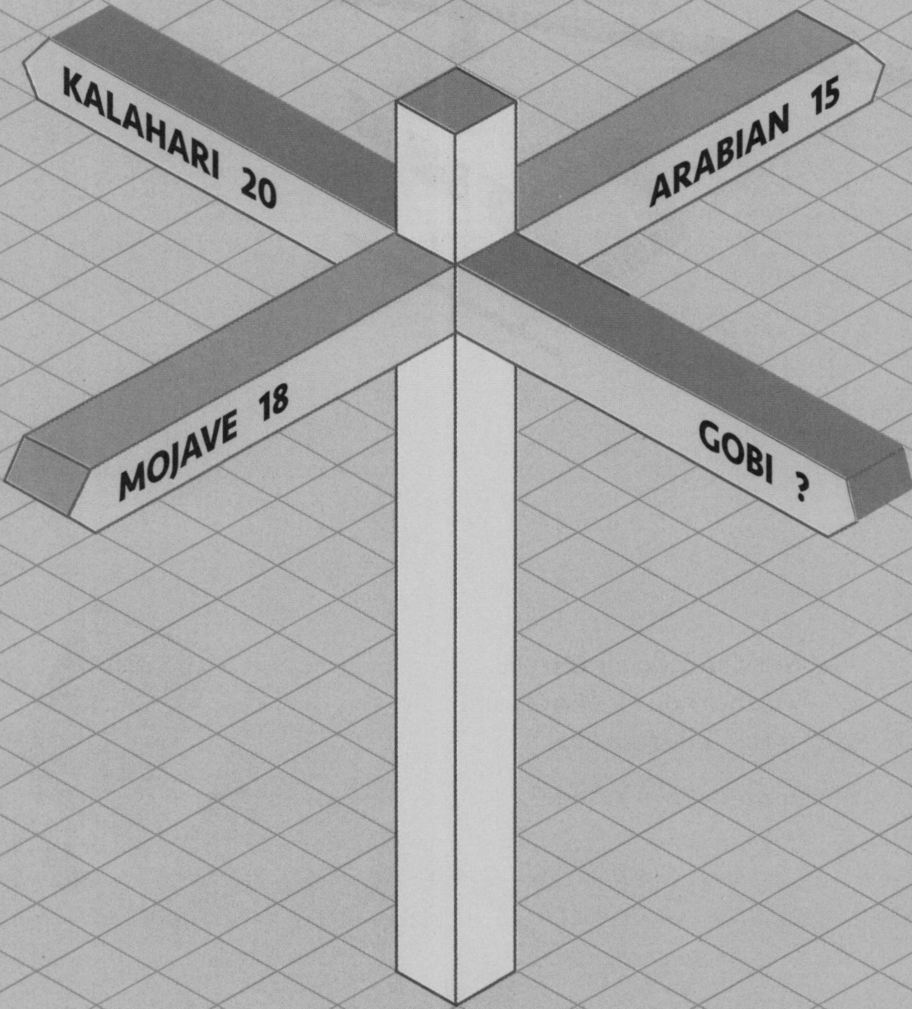

KALAHARI 20

ARABIAN 15

MOJAVE 18

GOBI ?

28

How many dashes should be contained on each row of the final box?

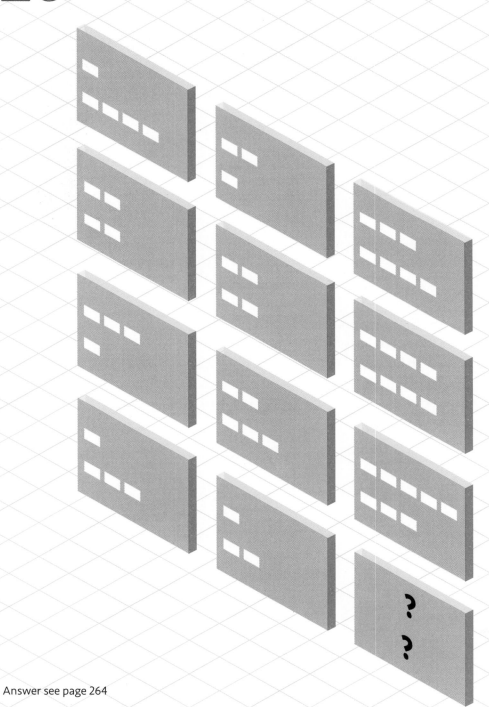

29

A hiker walks from one town to another. On the first day she covers two fifths of the total distance. The next day she covers one third of what is left. The following day she covers one quarter of the remainder and on the fourth day half of the remaining distance. She now has 12 miles left. How far has she walked?

Answer see page 265

30

The following numbers watch sports on television. How many watch hockey?

Boxing   – 11
Golf   – 50
Angling   – 51
Skiing   – 2
Cricket   – 201
Athletics – 151
Hockey   – **?**

Answer see page 265

31 **What number should replace the question mark?**

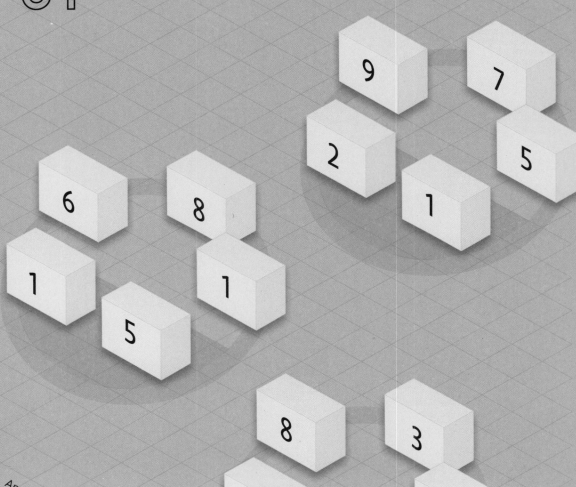

Answer see page 265

32 What number should replace the question mark in the grid?

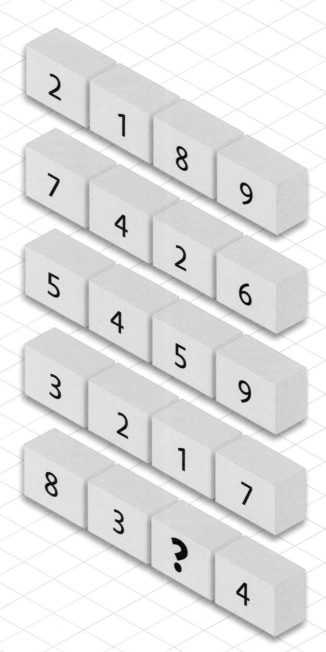

Answer see page 265

33 A truck and a van set off from the same point to travel the same journey. The truck sets off six minutes before the van. If the truck travels at 60 km/h and the van travels at 80 km/h, how many kilometres from the starting point will they draw level?

Answer see page 265

34 The sum of each two adjacent squares gives the number above. What number should replace the question mark?

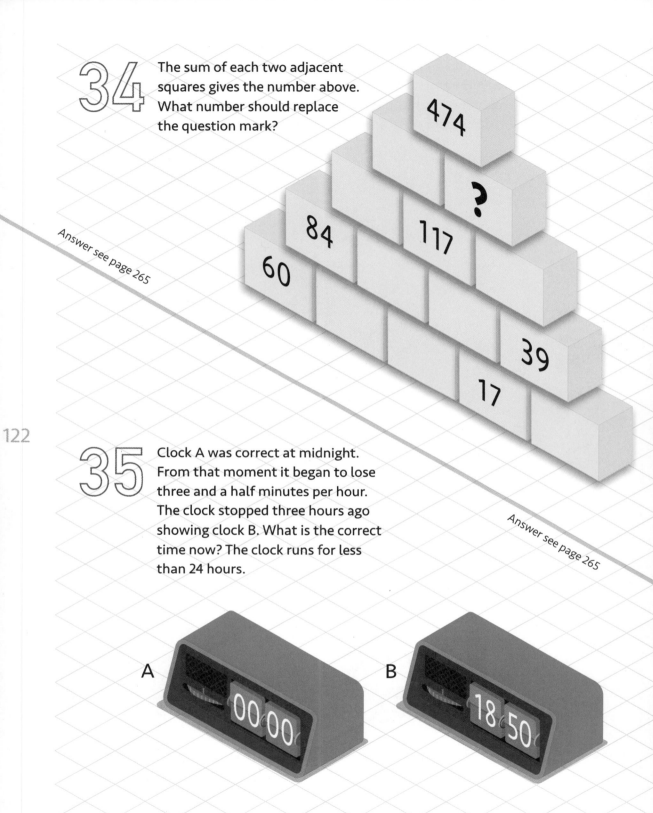

Answer see page 265

474

?

84 117

60

39

17

35 Clock A was correct at midnight. From that moment it began to lose three and a half minutes per hour. The clock stopped three hours ago showing clock B. What is the correct time now? The clock runs for less than 24 hours.

Answer see page 265

A 00:00

B 18:50

What is the value of the fourth column?

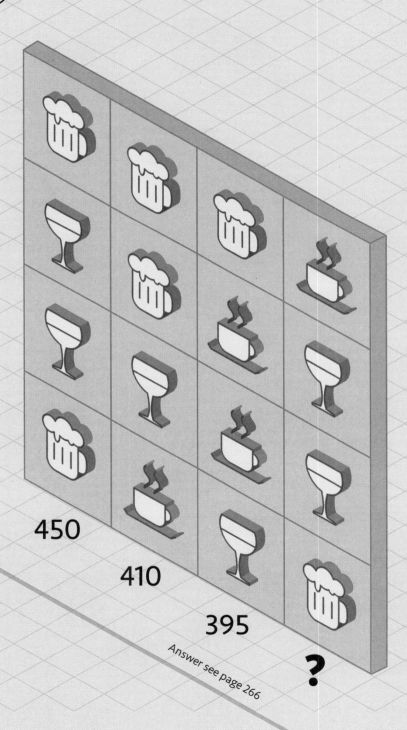

450

410

395

?

Answer see page 266

123

37 What number should replace the question mark?

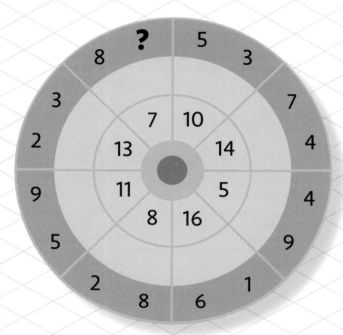

Answer see page 266

Answer see page 266

38 What number should replace the question mark?

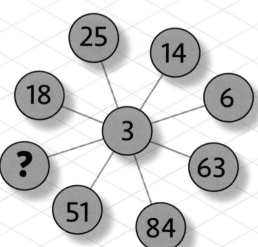

What numbers should replace the question marks?

9 27 12
16 64 20
6 30 11
15 ? ?

Answer see page 266

Answer see page 266

The sum of each two adjacent squares gives the number above. What number should replace the question mark?

175

?

9   48

1

22

15

A 440 yard long train, travelling at 60 mph, enters a one mile long tunnel. How long will elapse between the moment the front of the train enters the tunnel and the moment the end of the train clears the tunnel?

Answer see page 266

What number should replace the question mark in the circle?

Answer see page 266

126

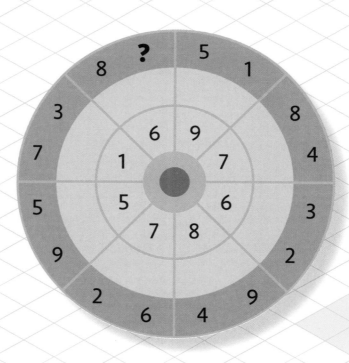

43

What number should replace the question mark?

Answer see page 267

93	6
32	1
51	4
74	3
85	?

44

What numbers should replace the question marks?

Answer see page 266

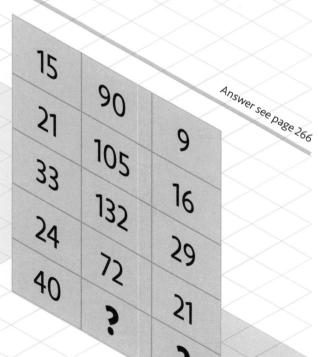

15	90	9
21	105	16
33	132	29
24	72	21
40	?	?

45

What is the value
of the fourth
column?

Answer see page 267

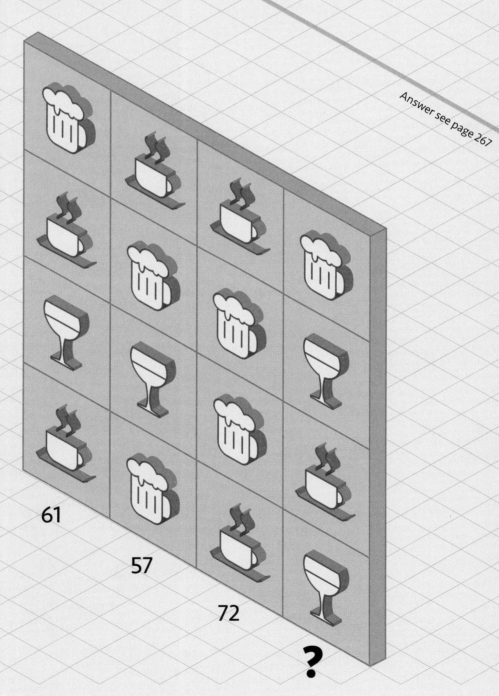

61

57

72

?

46 A train covers its outward journey at 110 mph. It returns, over exactly the same distance at 73.33 mph. What is the train's average speed over the entire journey?

Answer see page 267

Answer see page 267

47 What number should replace the question mark?

(34) (70)

(15) (32)

(11) (24)

(47) (96)

(29) (?)

48 A minibus and a coach set off from the same point, at the same time, to travel the same 140 mile journey. The minibus travels at 50 mph and the coach travels at 35 mph. What will be the difference in their arrival times?

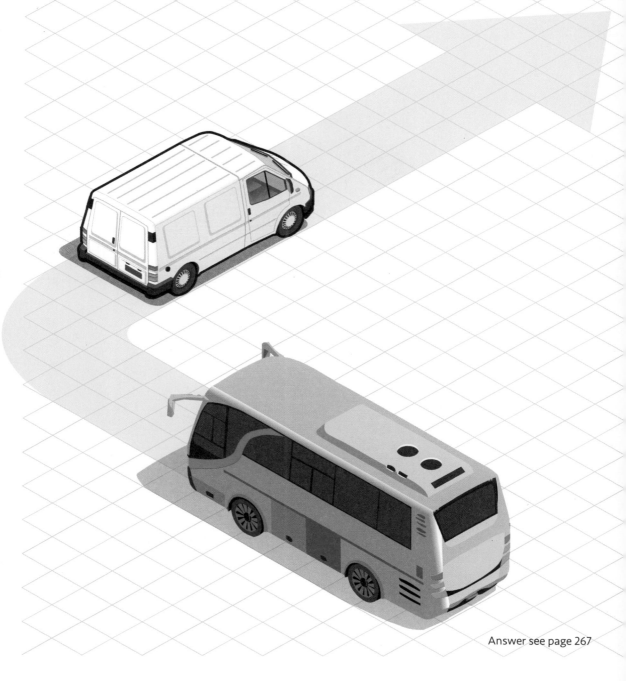

Answer see page 267

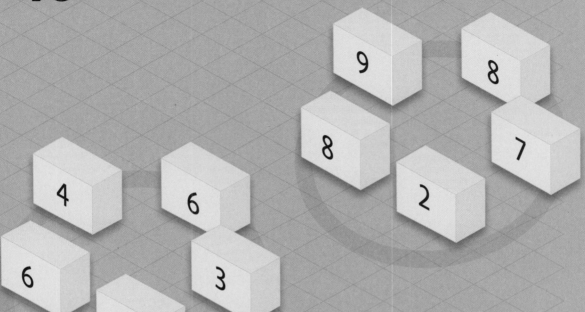

What number should replace the question mark?

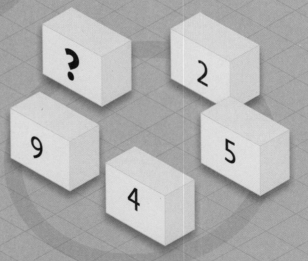

Answer see page 267

How many miles should it be to Amarillo on this signpost?

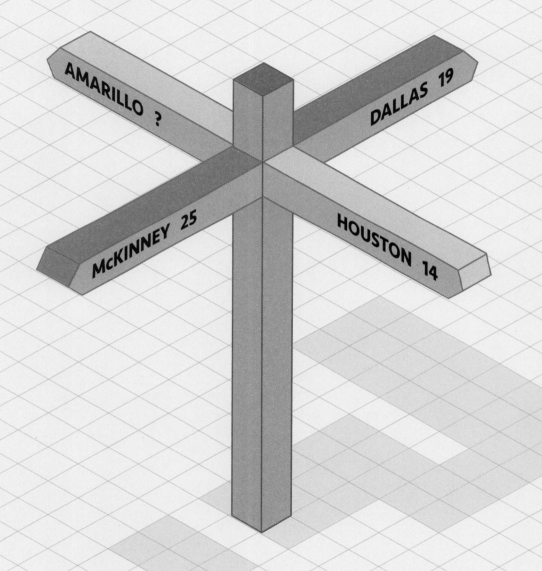

AMARILLO ?

DALLAS 19

McKINNEY 25

HOUSTON 14

Answer see page 267

Which is the missing box?

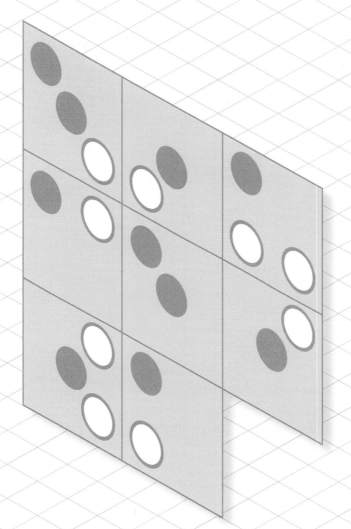

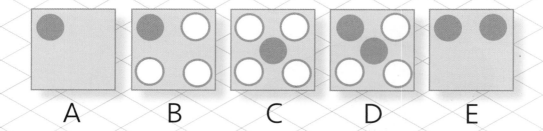

A   B   C   D   E

Answer see page 267

52 What number should replace the question mark?

17   8

56   11

32   5

12   3

84   ?

Answer see page 268

53 A car covers its outward journey at 35 mph. It returns, over exactly the same distance, at 26.25 mph. What is the car's average speed over the entire journey?

Answer see page 268

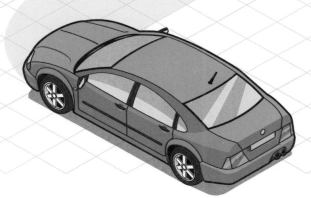

54 Which is the odd one out?

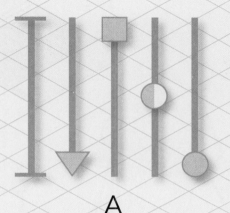

A

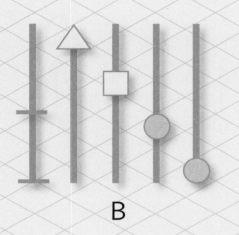

B

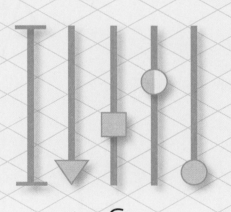

C

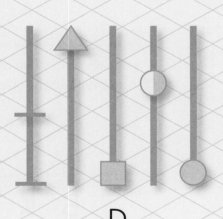

D

Answer see page 268

55

What would the next matchstick person in this sequence look like?

Answer see page 268

136

56

These pairs of circles obey a certain logic. What letter should replace the question mark?

Answer see page 268

B K

M

T G

D L

?

Q A

57 Which of the following circles' numbers cannot be rearranged into a seven-digit number that is perfectly divisible by 349?

A 1 4 4 7 1 1 4

B 0 0 6 7 8 0 0

C 0 3 3 7 4 4 0

D 1 2 4 7 1 2 4

E 2 4 4 7 1 1 4

Answer see page 268

58 Can you tell what number comes next in this sequence?

Answer see page 268

0 1 1 2 3 5 8 ?

Answer see page 268

59

The numbers in the cells represent the number of cells surrounding it that contain mines. Use logic to work out where the mines are placed.

1			2		1		1		1
	2			3				2	2
	1					2	2	3	
		2		2					2
2	2	1	0			2			
						2	1		
	2	1				2		3	
			1		2		1	2	
	3	2				2	2		3
2				2	1				

60

Given the five equations below, what is the value of x?

1. $(4x + 2y) / (a + b) = c$
2. $x^2 + a^2 = c^2 - 2y^2$
3. $3bx = 9y^2$
4. $a + c + 2y = 2b + x$
5. $2x + c = bx + a$

Answer see page 268

61

The numbers on each face of this cube, when arranged correctly, form 8-digit numbers which are the product of 6703 with another four-digit prime number. What are they?

Answer see page 269

62

A supplier sells boxes of dog biscuits in a range of sizes – 16, 17, 23, 24, 39, and 40 lbs, and will not split boxes. How would you order exactly 100 lbs of biscuits?

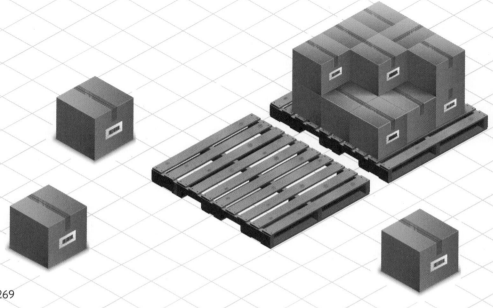

Answer see page 269

63

The following numbers are all types of what?

Answer see page 269

333336

500500

10011

66066

198765

According to the logic of these diagrams, what should replace the question mark?

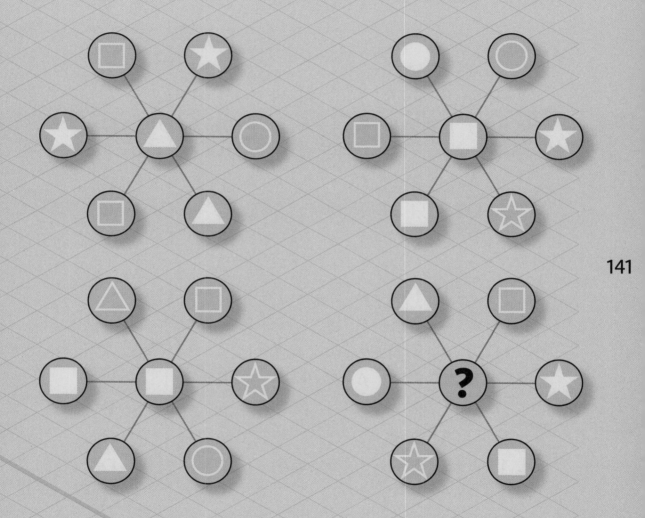

Answer see page 269

65 The word APHIDS is located exactly once in the grid below, but could be horizontally, vertically or diagonally forwards or backwards. Can you locate it?

Answer see page 269

```
H S S P S I S H H S I I A S S
S S D D H I I A D P A A D S D
A I I A P D H S D A I A A P I
I A H P H A I A A A P D P P D
P D P H H I H D S D D H D I A
A P A S P I S I D P P D D A I
I P A I D I I A H I A I S I I
P I I I I A P D P I S H H P S
H A A P D A H I A A A P I H P
H D A S I I D D A I A P S P A
S A S S D A A S I S S S I H H
D A I P P S H I I S H S D S P
S D S D A I D I P D A S I D S
I A S A I I A A S I A I H P D
I P A S D P I D S S S P D I H
```

66 This design works according to a specific logic. What should replace the question mark?

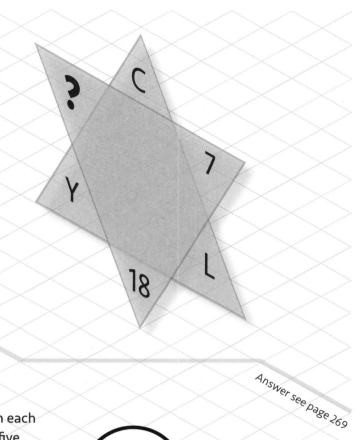

The star contains: ?, C, 7, L, 18, Y

Answer see page 269

Answer see page 269

67 Take one letter from each bulb in turn to find five cities. What are they?

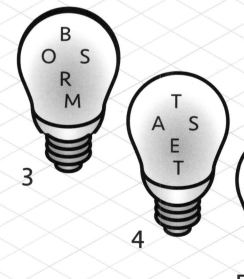

Bulb 3: B, O, S, R, M

Bulb 4: A, T, S, E, T

Bulb 1: D, E, K, P, T

Bulb 5: N, H, K, O, I

Bulb 2: S, O, Y, U, E

68 Following the logic of this grid, what number should replace the question mark?

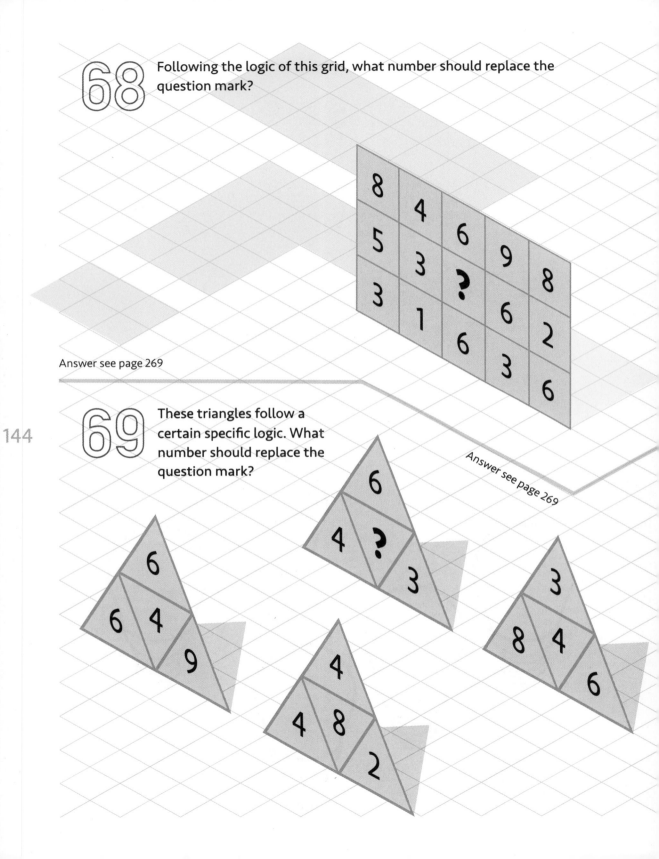

Answer see page 269

144

69 These triangles follow a certain specific logic. What number should replace the question mark?

Answer see page 269

70 This diagram follows a specific logic. What number should replace the question mark?

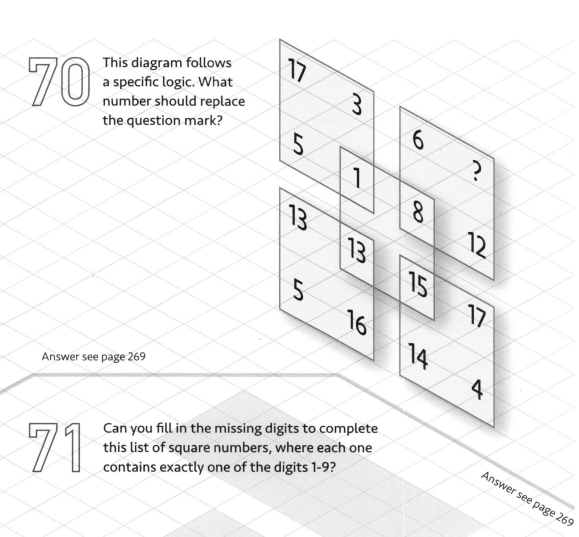

17
3
5
6
?
1
13
8
13
12
15
5
17
16
14
4

Answer see page 269

71 Can you fill in the missing digits to complete this list of square numbers, where each one contains exactly one of the digits 1-9?

Answer see page 269

	5	8	3	6	
	1	7	9	5	
	5	9	7	8	
	3	9	2	4	
	2	5	7	8	

72 The numbers in this diagram, starting at the top and progressing clockwise, represent a valid equation from which all mathematical operators have been removed. Please add back in +, −, * and / signs as necessary to make the equation valid, evaluating each sign's result strictly as you come to it.

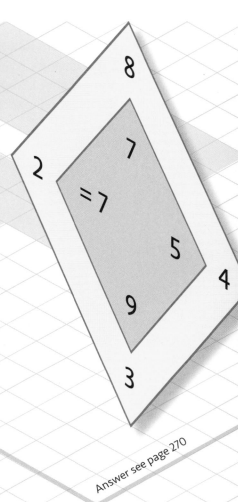

8

7

2

= 7

5

4

9

3

Answer see page 270

146

Answer see page 270

73 The following numbers obey a certain logic. What number should replace the question mark?

A	B	C	D	E
8	5	9	5	3
3	3	8	9	6
7	0	0	9	7
0	3	6	6	3
2	4	6	9	?
		3	1	

74 The symbols in this design appear in a certain order. Which should replace the question mark?

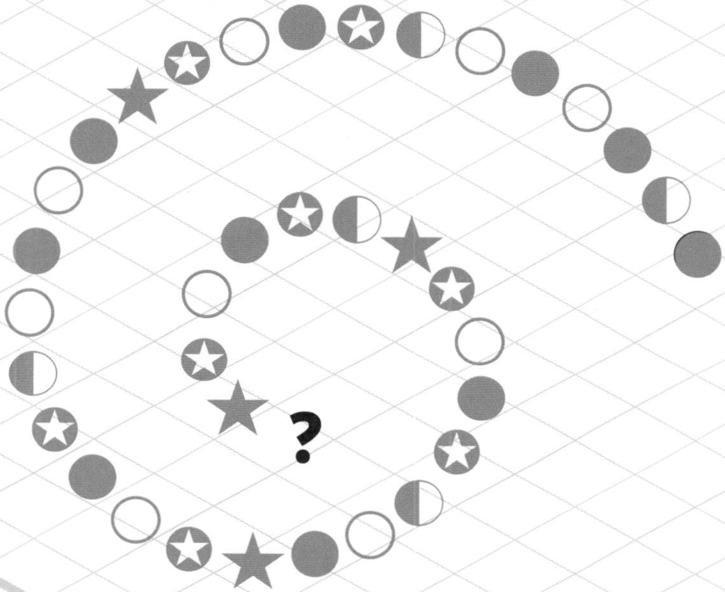

Answer see page 270

Answer see page 270

75 Six of these seven numbers are logically related. Which is the odd one out?

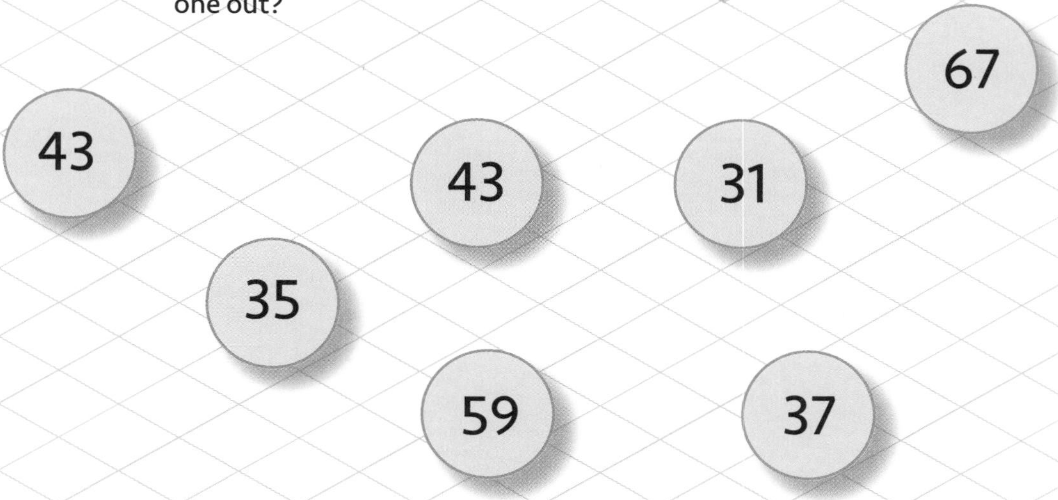

67

43

43

31

35

59

37

Logically, which letter in the second circle should be in the first circle?

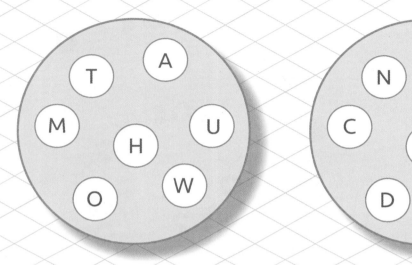

Answer see page 270

77 This grid obeys a certain logic. What number should replace the question mark?

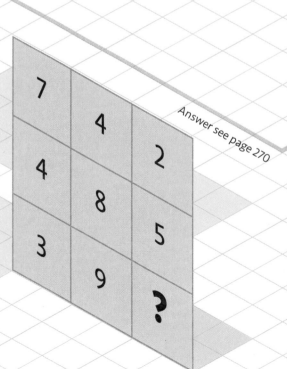

Answer see page 270

78 There are certain numbers missing from this jumbled list. What do they have in common?

54 44 33 34 52 38

39 30 51 36 42 49

40 32 48 35 45 50 46

Answer see page 270

Answer see page 270

79 Following on from the other three clocks, what should be the time on the fourth?

A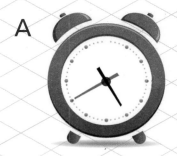

B

C

D

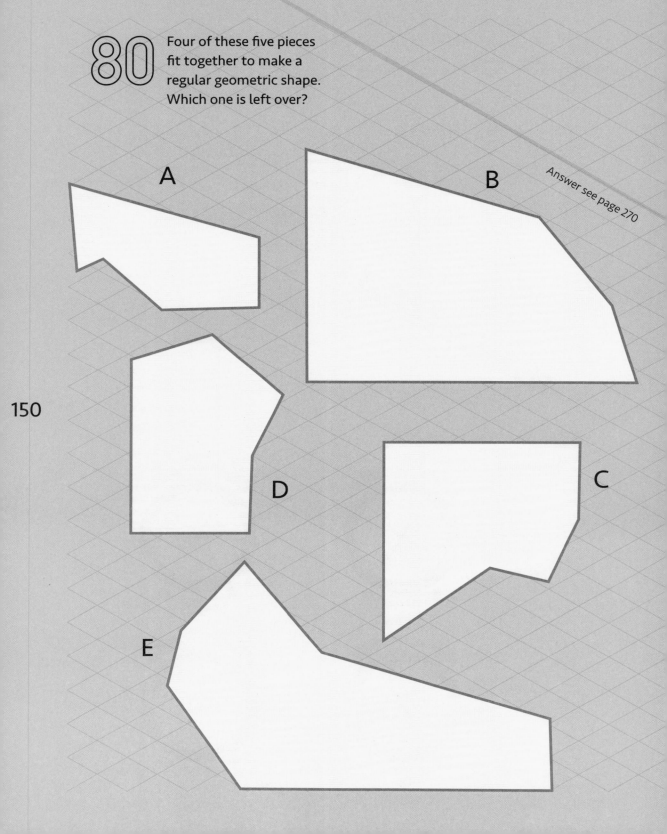

Four of these five pieces
fit together to make a
regular geometric shape.
Which one is left over?

Answer see page 270

A

B

150

D

C

E

81 Can you uncover the logic of this grid of letters and replace the question mark with the right letter?

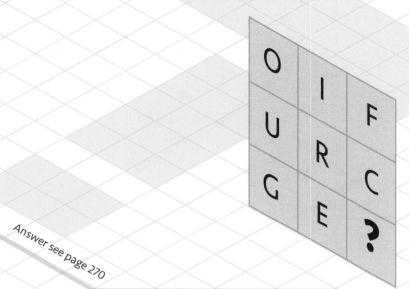

Answer see page 270

82 Moving from circle to circle without backtracking, can you find a ten-digit square number that uses each digit once?

Answer see page 270

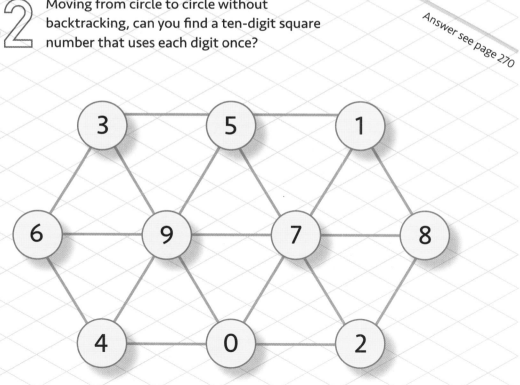

83

The equation spelled out with matchsticks below is correct. Can you move just two matchsticks to form another correct equation?

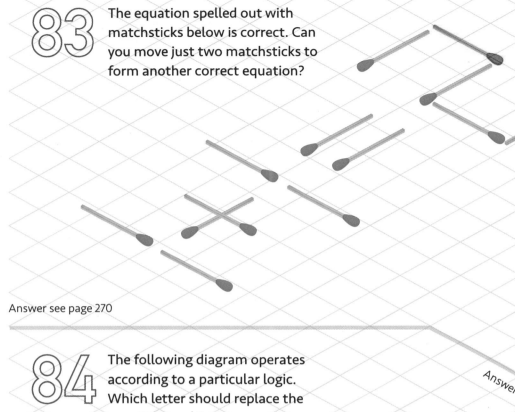

Answer see page 270

84

The following diagram operates according to a particular logic. Which letter should replace the question mark?

Answer see page 270

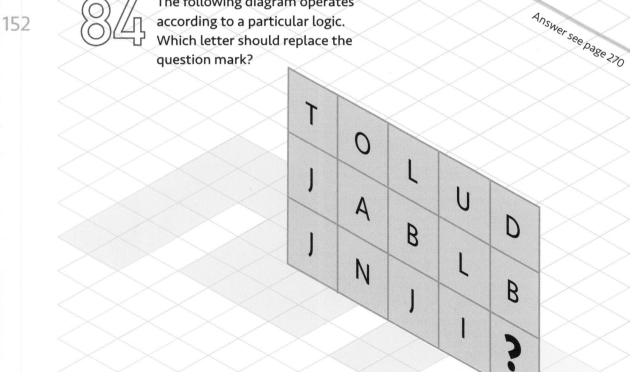

T	O	L	U	D
J	A	B	L	B
J	N	J	I	?

These circles function according to a certain logic. What number should replace the question mark?

B

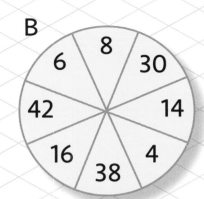

A

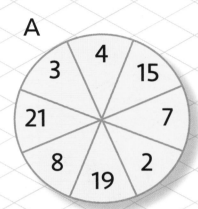

C

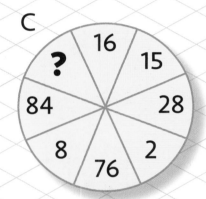

Answer see page 271

All the mathematical symbols have been removed from this balanced equation. Can you reconstitute it?

Answer see page 271

23 ◯ 8 ◯ 1 ◯ 10 ◯ 5 ◯ 8 ◯ 2 ◯ 1

87

Which pair of sides
contain the same
roman numbers?

Answer see page 271

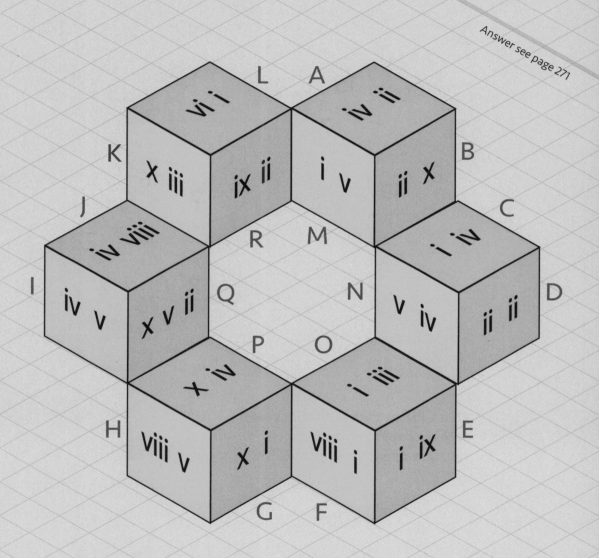

88 What is the missing number?

11
45
25
27
23
39
5
36
14
18
32
?

Answer see page 271

Answer see page 271

89 There is a pattern behind these dominoes.
What should replace the question mark?

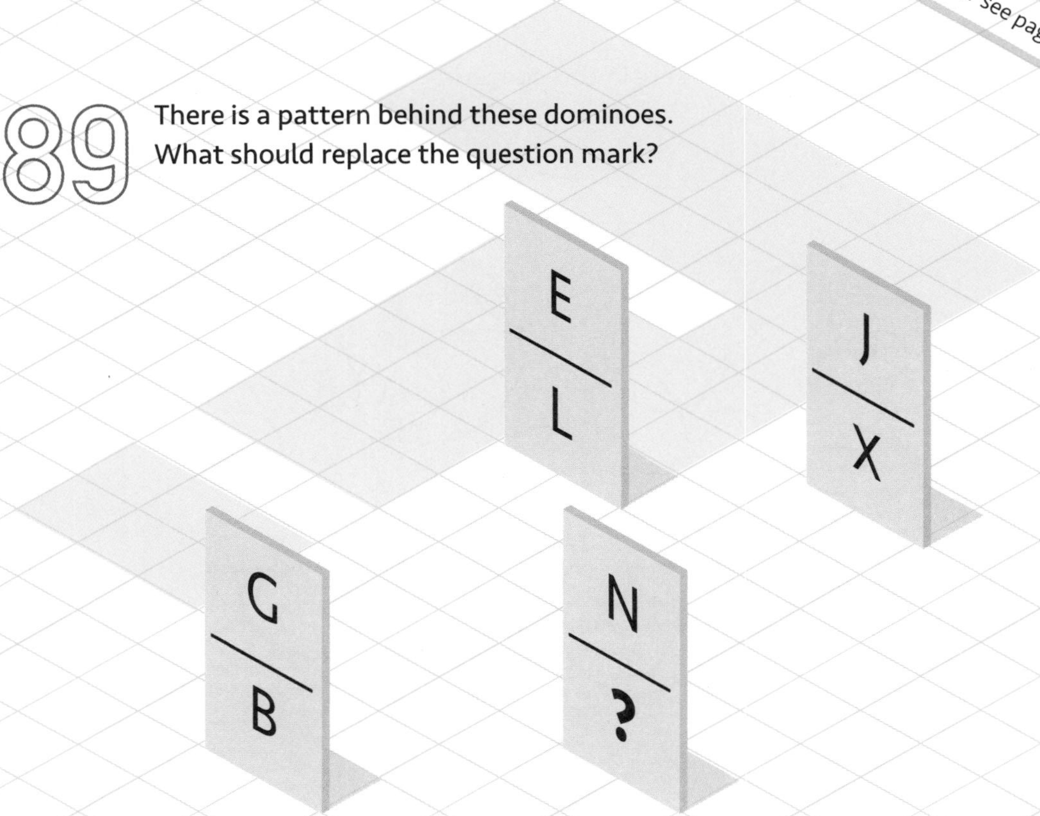

$\frac{E}{L}$

$\frac{J}{X}$

$\frac{G}{B}$

$\frac{N}{?}$

90 Either multiplying or dividing by a single-digit integer each time, and making sure each result is between 0 and 9999, can you get from the top number to the bottom number using precisely three intermediate steps?

1	0	2	4
2	6	8	8

Answer see page 271

Answer see page 271

156

91 How many circles are in this congeries?

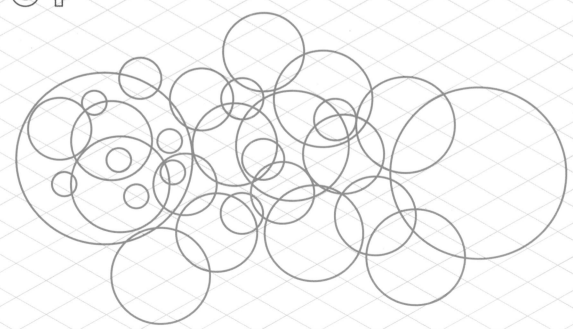

Answer see page 271

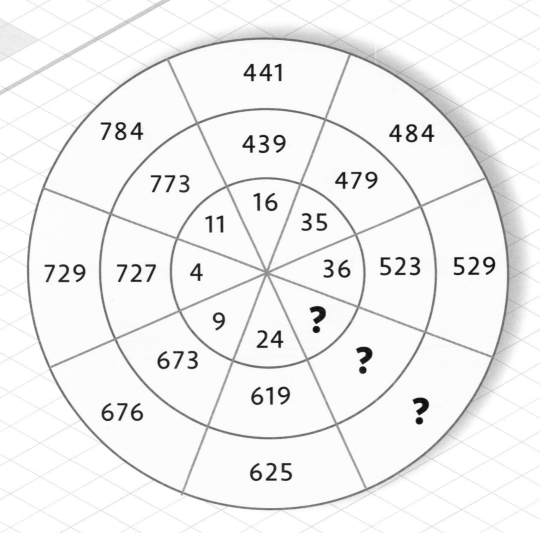

92 In the above diagram, what numbers should replace the question marks?

93

The dots on this grid have been filled according to a specific logic. One filled dot has been left out. Where should it go?

158

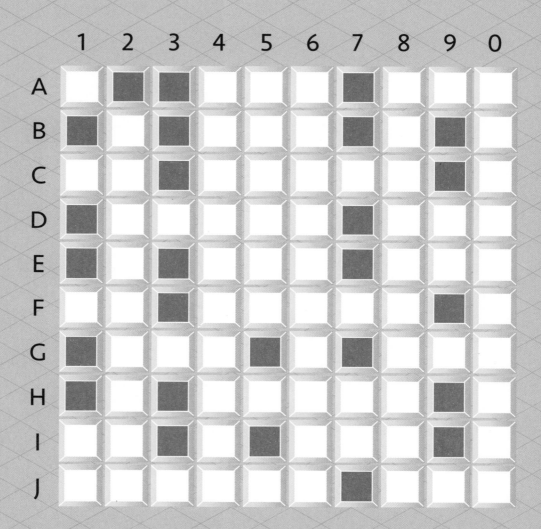

Answer see page 271

The numbers in this list are sequential terms in a specific sequence of numbers, but they are out of order. What is the sequence?

1 2 1 3 9 3
1 3 4 6 2 6 9
1 9 6 4 1 8
2 1 7 8 3 0 9
3 1 7 8 1 1
3 5 2 4 5 7 8
4 6 3 6 8
5 1 4 2 2 9
7 5 0 2 5
8 3 2 0 4 0

Answer see page 271

159

Answer see page 271

The Roman numeral equation spelled out with matchsticks below is incorrect. Can you move just one matchstick to form a correct equation?

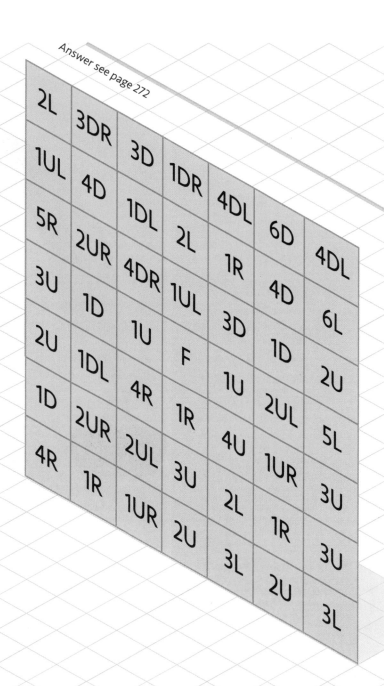

96 Each square on this grid shows you the move you must make to arrive at the next square in the sequence, Left, Right, Up, and/or Down. So 3R would be three squares right, and 4UL would be 4 squares diagonally up and left. Your goal is to end up on the finish square, F, having visited every square exactly once. Can you find the starting square?

97 These circles obey a certain logic. Knowing that, what letter should replace the question mark?

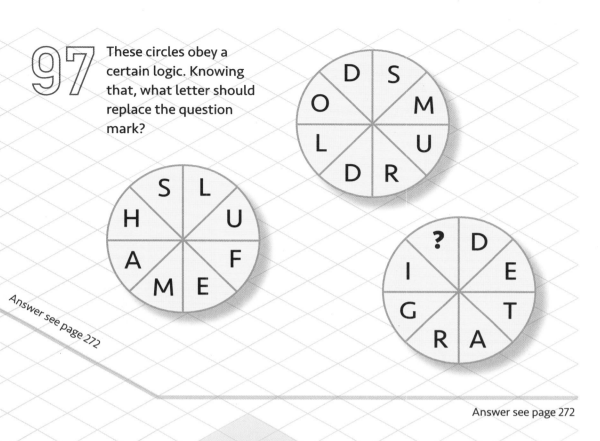

Answer see page 272

Answer see page 272

98 These dominos obey a certain logic. What should replace the question mark?

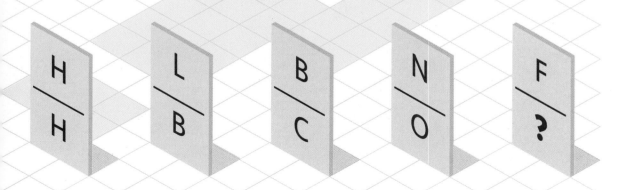

99 Delete all instances of letters that appear more than once, and rearrange the remainder to find the name of a city. What is it?

E P L A D Q S X
F P L T I H G H
M N Y T T O B W
Q J G Z I X U C
D K R O I K F F
J X S V M W Y B

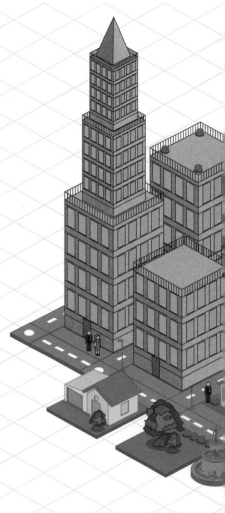

Answer see page 272

100 In this irregular magic square, every row, column and five-figure diagonal adds to 115. The blank spaces each need to be filled by one of four numbers. Can you complete the square?

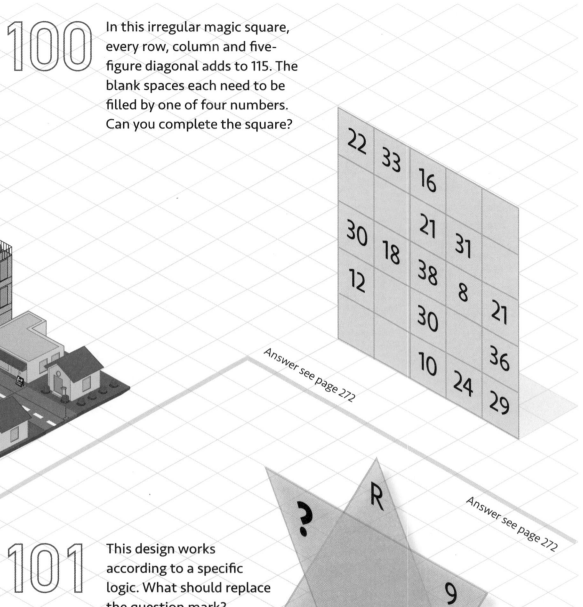

22	33	16		
30	18	21	31	
12		38	8	21
		30		21
		10	24	36

Answer see page 272

Answer see page 272

101 This design works according to a specific logic. What should replace the question mark?

?

R

9

L

F

4

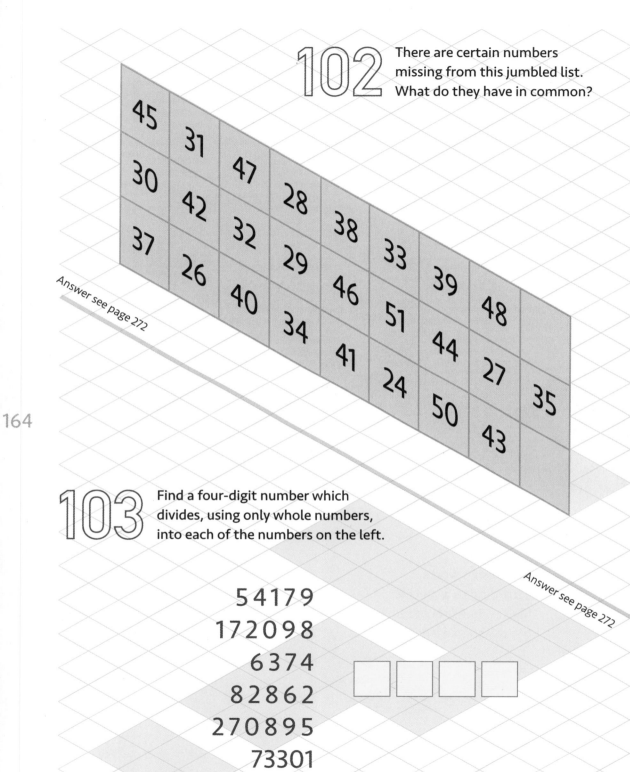

102 There are certain numbers missing from this jumbled list. What do they have in common?

45 31 47 30 42 28 32 38 37 26 29 33 39 40 46 48 34 51 44 41 24 27 35 50 43

Answer see page 272

103 Find a four-digit number which divides, using only whole numbers, into each of the numbers on the left.

54179
172098
6374
82862
270895
73301

Answer see page 272

The following diagram obeys a specific logic.
What should replace the question mark?

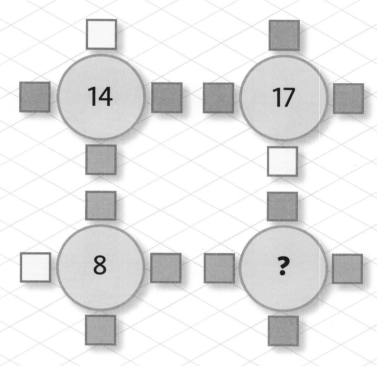

165

Answer see page 272

Answer see page 272

105

You have a coin that is biased, and
does not generate heads and tails
with equal probability. How can
you use it to make an unbiased
either/or decision?

106

Can you fill in the numbers provided to correctly complete the grid?

3 digit numbers	420	4 digit numbers	7 digit numbers	9 digit numbers
183	483	3327	1277149	168357562
212	534	6433		233571289
256	584	8021	8 digit numbers	391368944
301	598			596682946
342	619	6 digit numbers	84332386	860352417
374	660		89239583	974132425
376	876	266447		
409	933	749394		
	972			

This grid obeys a specific sequence. However, some numbers are out of order. When shaded in, these will reveal another number. What is it?

6	3	8	0	1	2	5	0	3
1	4	3	6	3	8	2	5	2
5	1	4	1	4	3	6	3	5
0	1	0	5	0	3	1	4	3
6	3	5	0	1	2	5	0	4
1	4	3	6	3	8	0	1	0
5	0	4	1	4	0	6	3	1
0	1	0	5	0	3	0	6	0
6	3	1	0	1	2	5	0	6
1	4	3	6	3	8	0	1	0
5	0	4	1	4	0	6	3	1
0	1	0	5	0	3	1	4	3
6	0	1	0	1	2	4	5	3
1	4	0	6	3	8	0	1	2

108

Two moons are orbiting a planet. One takes 16 days to make a full circuit. The other takes 9 days. If they are now in a perfect conjunction, with the quicker moon directly in between the planet and the slower moon, when will the three celestial bodies next be in a straight line?

Answer see page 273

270

315

225

180

135

90

109

The letters on this cube, when correctly assembled, spell out the name of a novel and its author. What is it?

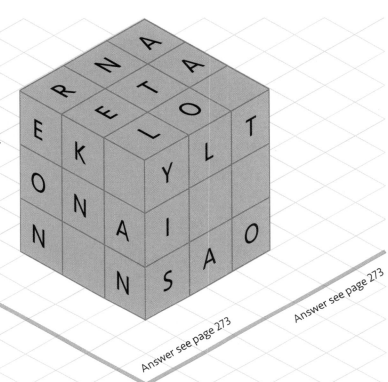

Answer see page 273
Answer see page 273

110

These triangles obey a certain logic. What letter should replace the question mark?

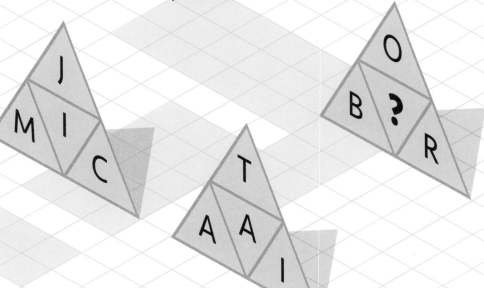

111

Can you fill in the missing digits to complete this list of square numbers, where each one contains exactly one of the digits 1-9?

	2	9	3	8	
	4	1	9	3	
	2	1	7	5	
	1	3	4	7	
	3	2	9	8	

Answer see page 273

112

What should replace the question mark in the final square?

Answer see page 273

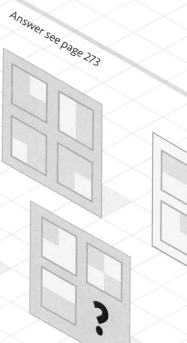

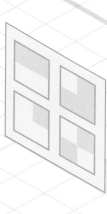

113 Examine the following sets of scales, which are in perfect balance. How many squares are needed to balance the final scale?

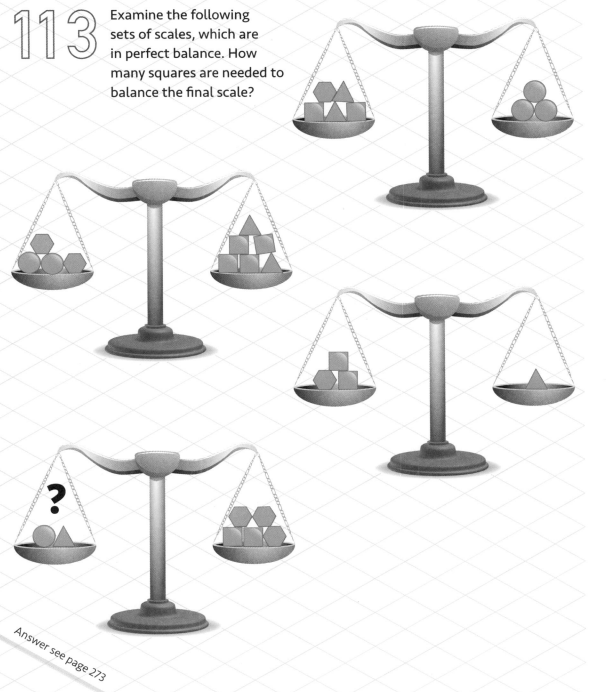

Answer see page 273

DIFFICULT PUZZLES

Complete the square with the numbers 1 – 5 so that no row, column or diagonal line of any length contains the same number more than once. What number should replace the question mark?

Answer see page 276

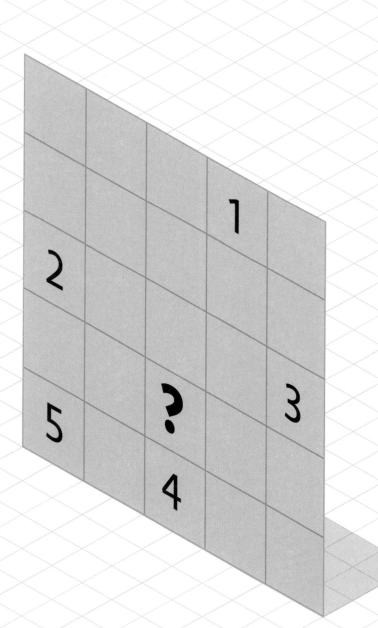

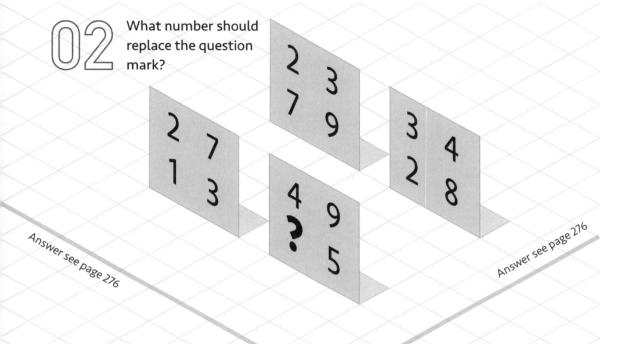

02 What number should replace the question mark?

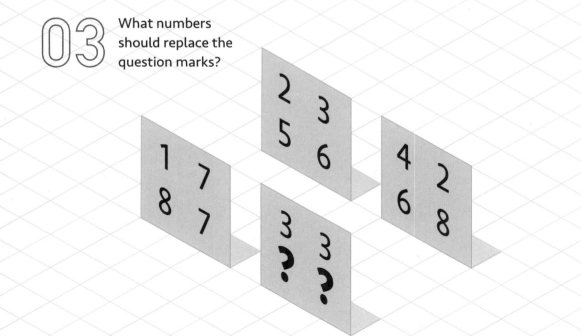

03 What numbers should replace the question marks?

Answer see page 276

Answer see page 276

04

At a leisure centre there are three times as many people swimming as there are boxing. 12 more people are doing aerobics than boxing and 11 less people are playing badminton than doing aerobics. 10 people are playing badminton, how many are doing each of the other sports?

Answer see page 276

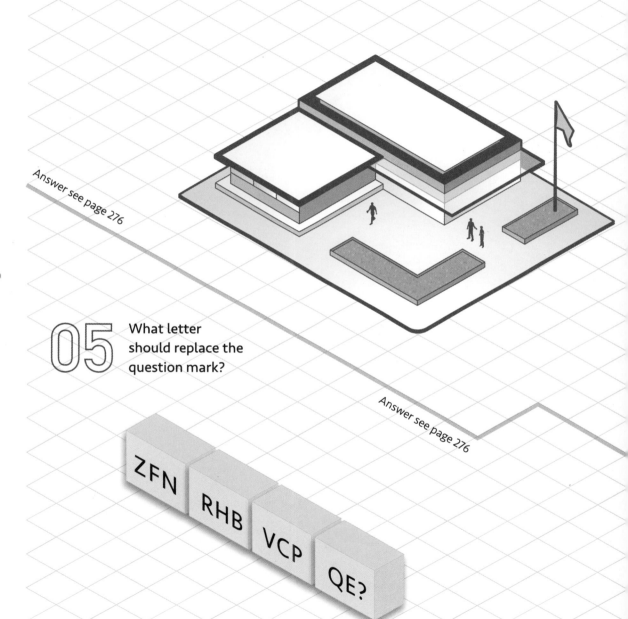

05

What letter should replace the question mark?

Answer see page 276

ZFN RHB VCP QE?

What number should replace the question mark?

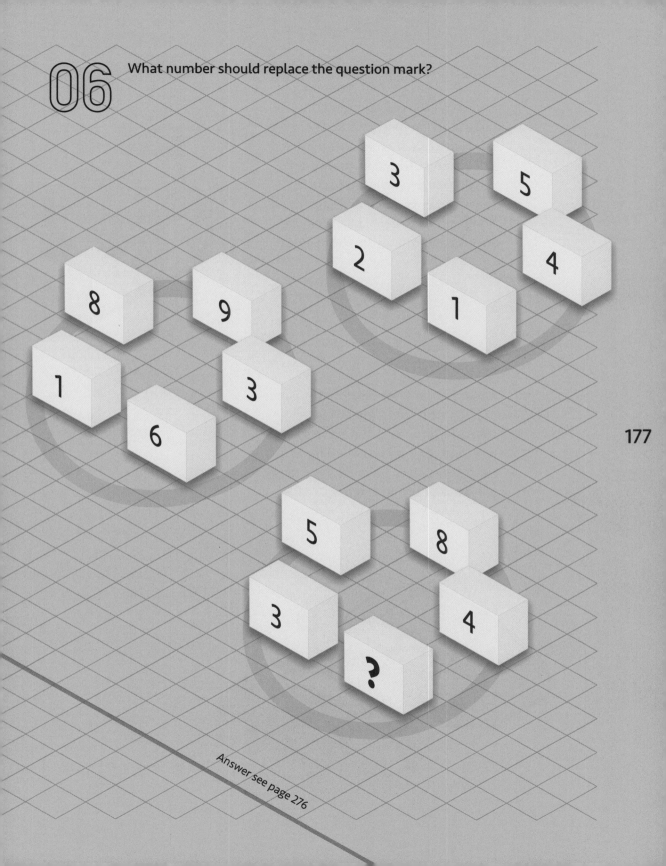

3

5

2

4

1

8

9

1

4

1

3

6

177

5

8

3

4

?

07

A customer pays $16.80 in a store. She pays in four different denominations of coins and the largest denomination is $1. She pays with exactly the same number of each coin. The coins that could possibly be available are 1 cent, 5 cents, 10 cents, 25 cents, 50 cents and 1 dollar, how many of each coin did she use and what were their values?

Answer see page 276

08

Car A and car B set off from the same point, at the same time, to travel the same journey. Car A travels at 50 mph and car B travels at 40 mph. If car A stops after 115 miles, how long will it take car B to catch up?

Answer see page 276

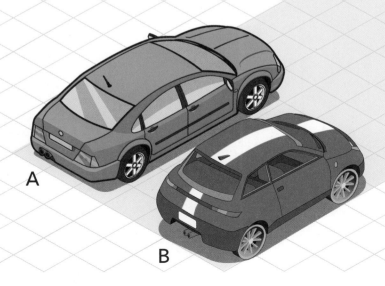

A

B

What number should replace the question mark in the grid?

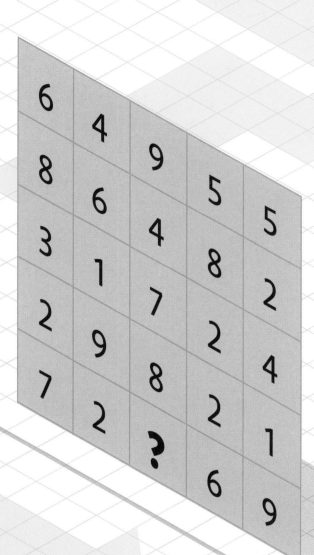

Answer see page 276

10 Should A, B or C
continue the sequence?

Answer see page 277

A

B

C

11 Which number is the odd one out?

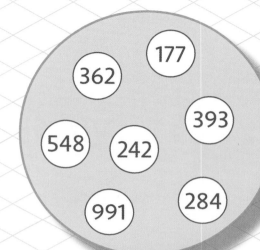

Answer see page 277

Answer see page 277

12 Assume you are using a basic calculator and apply the mathematical operations strictly in the order chosen. Replace each question mark with a mathematical sign. Plus, minus, multiply and divide can each be used once only.

What are the highest and lowest numbers you can possibly score?

4 ? 2 ? 8 ? 3 ? 5 = ?

13

Assume you are using a basic calculator and apply the mathematical operations strictly in the order chosen. Replace each question mark with a mathematical sign. Plus, minus, multiply and divide can each be used once only. In what order should they be used to score minus 42?

$$2 \;?\; 6 \;?\; 8 \;?\; 3 \;?\; 9 = -42$$

Answer see page 277

14

Which number is the odd one out?

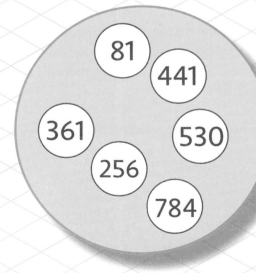

81
441
361
256
530
784

Answer see page 277

15 A 110 yard long train, travelling at 30 mph, enters a three mile long tunnel. How long will elapse between the moment the front of the train enters the tunnel and the moment the end of the train clears the tunnel?

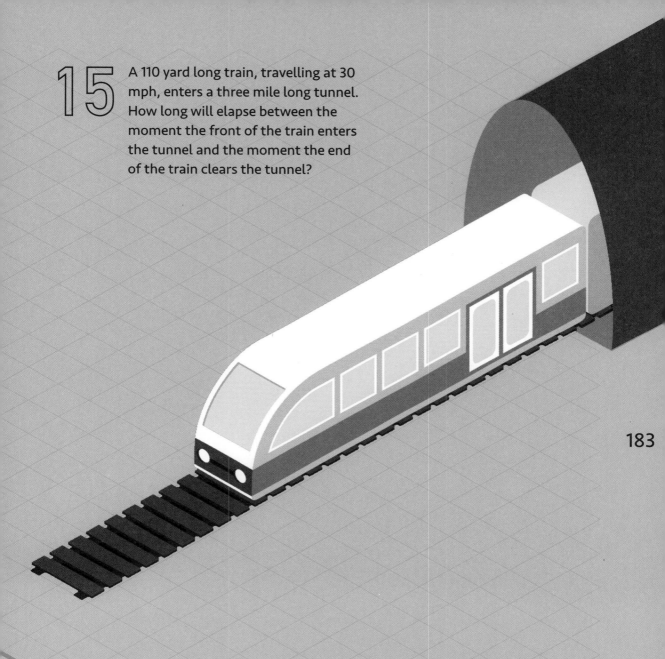

Answer see page 277

16

Which is the odd one out?

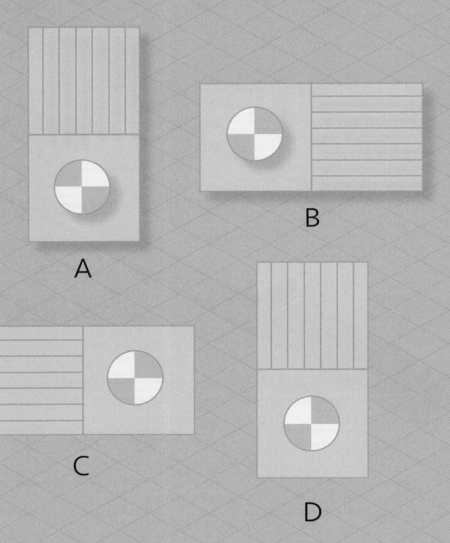

A

B

C

D

Answer see page 277

17 What number should replace the question mark?

7

3   2

8   2

2   4   ?

9

5

Answer see page 277

18 A car has travelled 80 miles at 40 mph. It started its journey with 10 gallons of fuel but its tank has been leaking throughout the journey and is now dry. The car completes 40 miles per gallon. How many gallons of fuel does it leak per hour?

Answer see page 277

What number should replace the question mark?

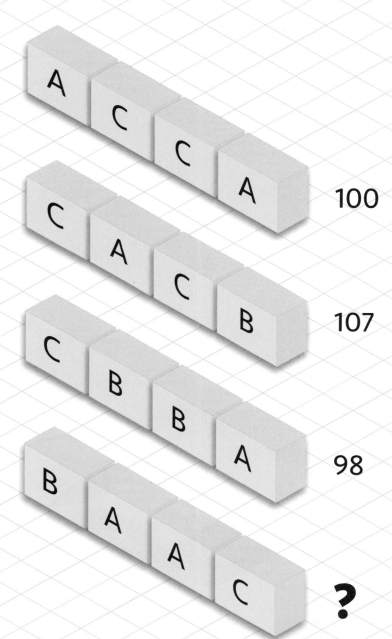

Answer see page 277

20

Two vehicles set off from the same point to travel the same journey. The first vehicle sets off nine minutes before the second vehicle. If the first vehicle travels at 85 km/h and the second vehicle travels at 100 km/h, how many kilometres from the starting point will the two vehicles draw level?

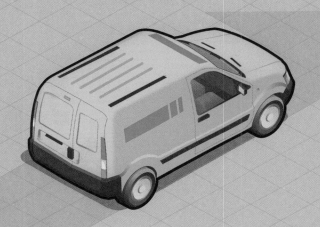

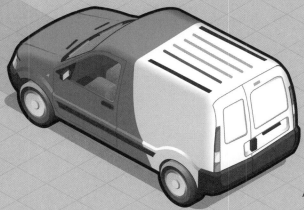

Answer see page 278

21 A group were discussing where to eat. Four times as many wanted Italian food as wanted Chinese. Five more people chose Indian than chose Chinese and three less people opted for Thai than for Indian. Four people wanted Thai food, how many chose Italian, how many chose Chinese and how many chose Indian?

Answer see page 278

Answer see page 278

22 What number should replace the question mark?

27 19 35

24 18 30

14 10 18

13 11 ?

23

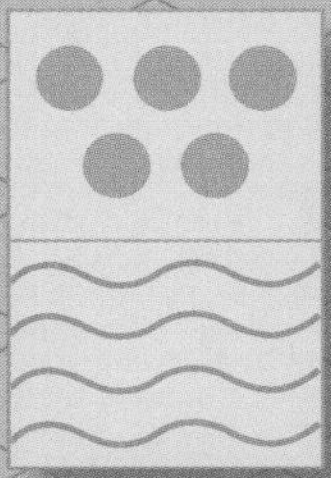

is to

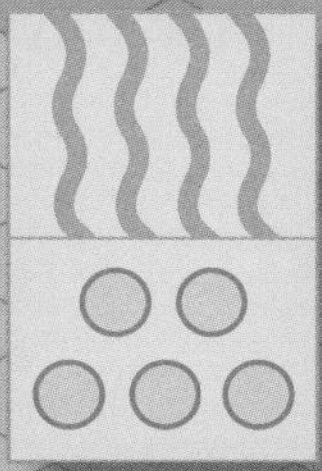

as

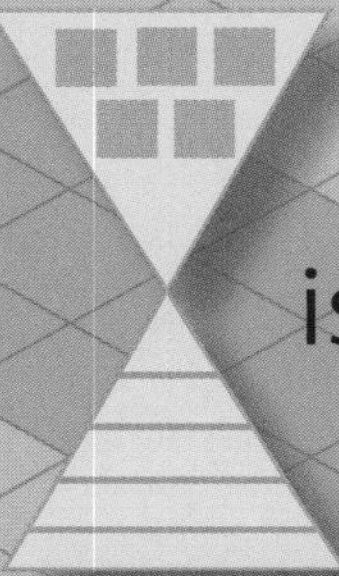

is to

A

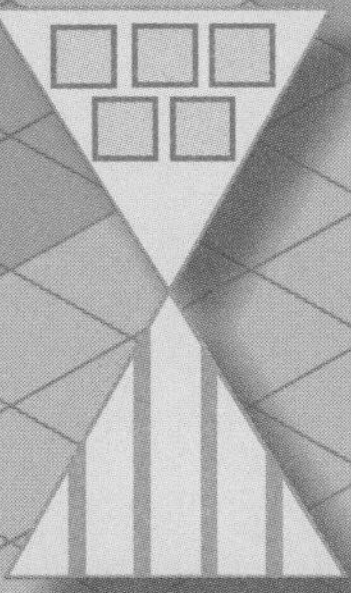

B

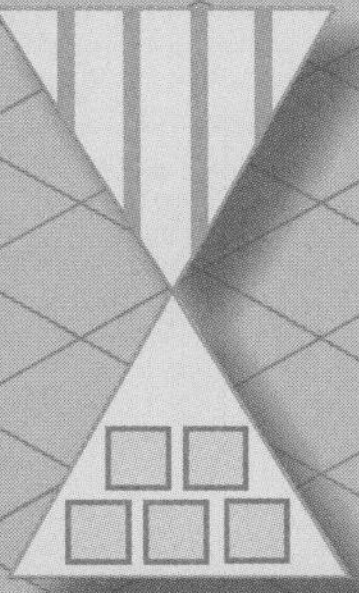

C

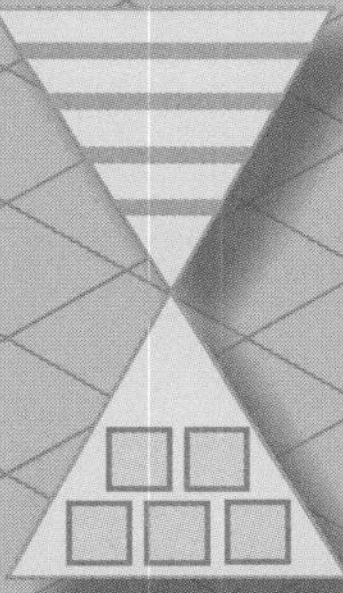

Answer see page 278

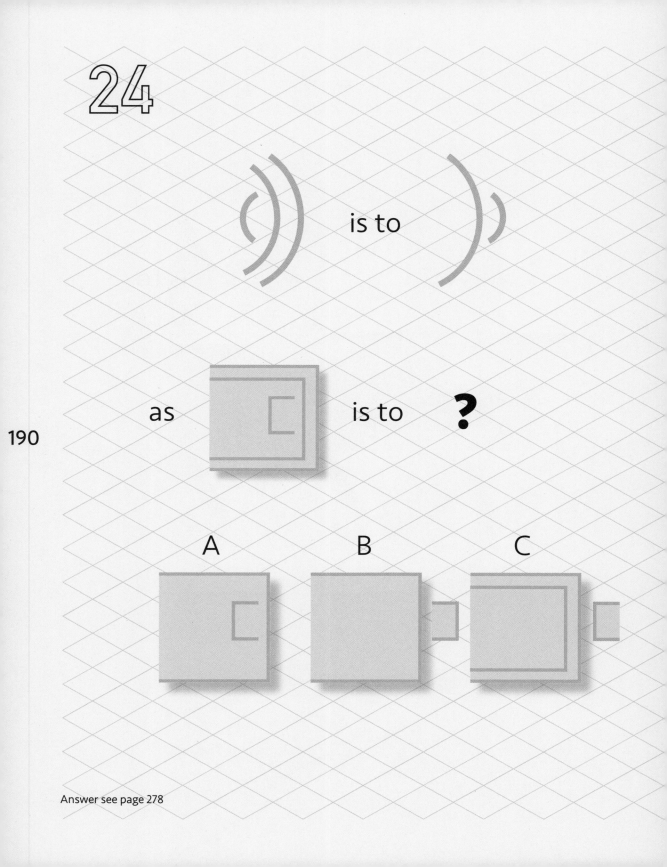

is to

as

is to

?

A

B

C

Answer see page 278

25 A fire engine travels nine miles to a fire at a speed of 32 mph. Its tank holds 500 gallons of water but has been leaking throughout the journey at a rate of 20 gallons per hour.

If the fire engine needs 496 gallons of water to put out the fire, will it succeed?

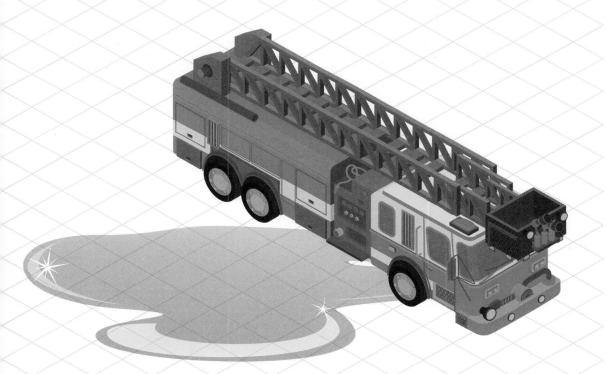

Answer see page 278

26 Clock A was correct at midnight. From that moment it began to lose one minute per hour. The clock stopped 90 minutes ago showing clock B. What is the correct time now? The clock runs for less than 24 hours.

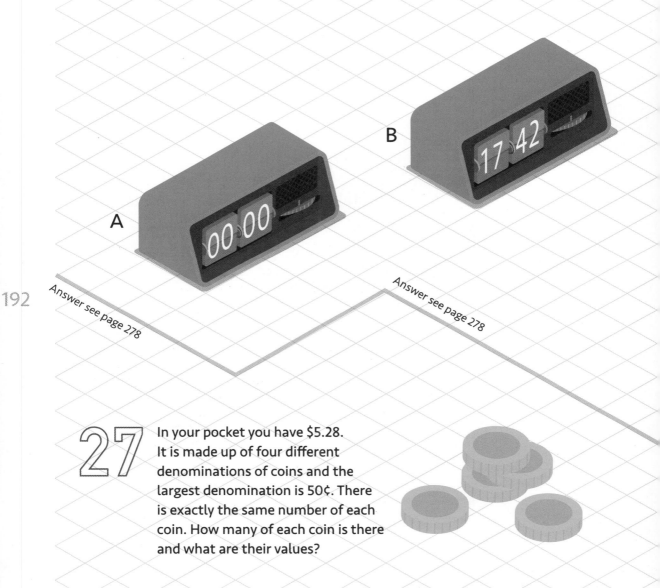

B

A

Answer see page 278

Answer see page 278

27 In your pocket you have $5.28. It is made up of four different denominations of coins and the largest denomination is 50¢. There is exactly the same number of each coin. How many of each coin is there and what are their values?

28

is to

as

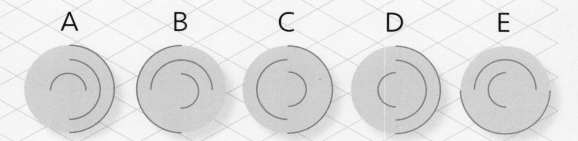

is to

?

A B C D E

Answer see page 278

29

Should A, B, or C continue the sequence?

Answer see page 279

194

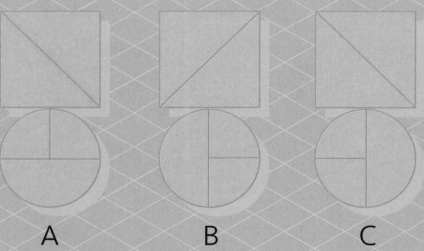

A   B   C

30 A boy is practising throwing a ball through a basketball hoop. In the first 20 minutes he is successful an average of twice every minute. After a further 25 minutes practising, his average stands at seven successes per minute. What is the boy's average number of successful shots per minute of the last 25 minutes only?

Answer see page 279

31 Add together three of the following numbers each time to score 20. Each number can be used as many times as you wish. How many different combinations are there?

Answer see page 279

2   4   6   8   10   12   14

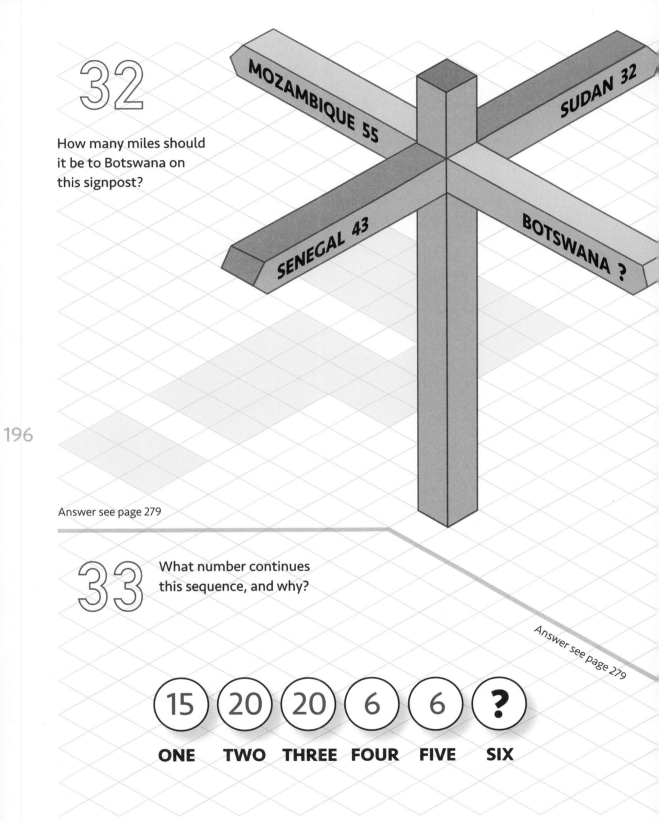

32

How many miles should it be to Botswana on this signpost?

MOZAMBIQUE 55

SUDAN 32

SENEGAL 43

BOTSWANA ?

Answer see page 279

33

What number continues this sequence, and why?

Answer see page 279

15	20	20	6	6	?
ONE	TWO	THREE	FOUR	FIVE	SIX

The following grid operates according to a specific pattern.
Can you fill in the blank section?

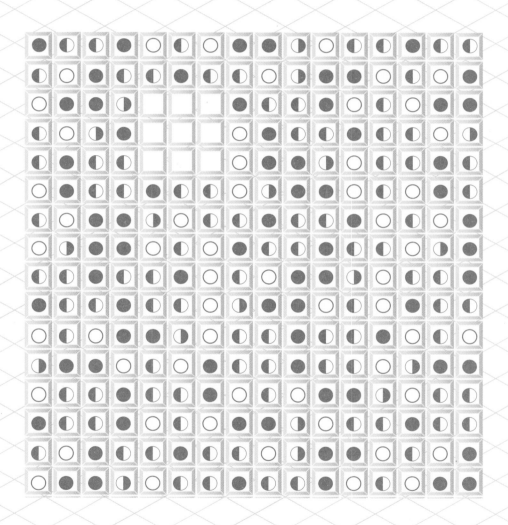

Answer see page 280

Answer see page 280

35

The numbers in the cells represent the number of cells surrounding it that contain mines. Use logic to work out where the mines are placed.

1				2			4				
	3	3	3		3	3			4	2	2
						2					
		3	3		2		1				
2										2	
0			2	2		0	2				2
			1	1				2	3		
1							0	0			
2	3				1					3	
	3			2			1	1	3		2
			3	3					4		2
	2	0			2	1				2	

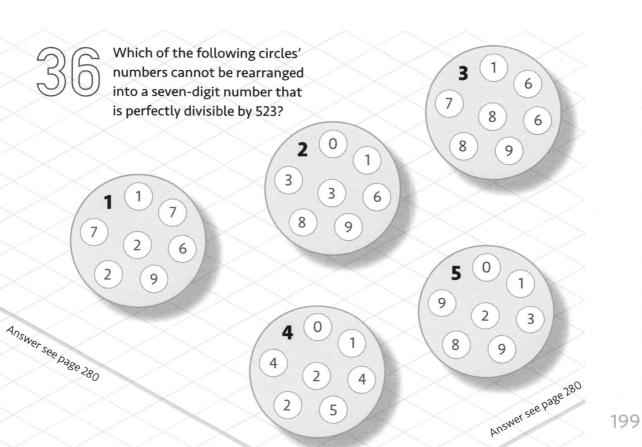

36 Which of the following circles' numbers cannot be rearranged into a seven-digit number that is perfectly divisible by 523?

1 1 7 7 2 6 2 9

2 0 1 3 3 6 8 9

3 1 6 7 8 6 8 9

4 0 1 4 2 4 2 5

5 0 1 9 2 3 8 9

Answer see page 280

Answer see page 280

37 All the mathematical symbols have been removed from this balanced equation. Can you reconstitute it?

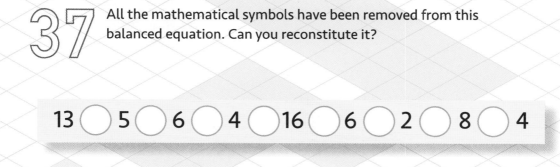

13 ◯ 5 ◯ 6 ◯ 4 ◯ 16 ◯ 6 ◯ 2 ◯ 8 ◯ 4

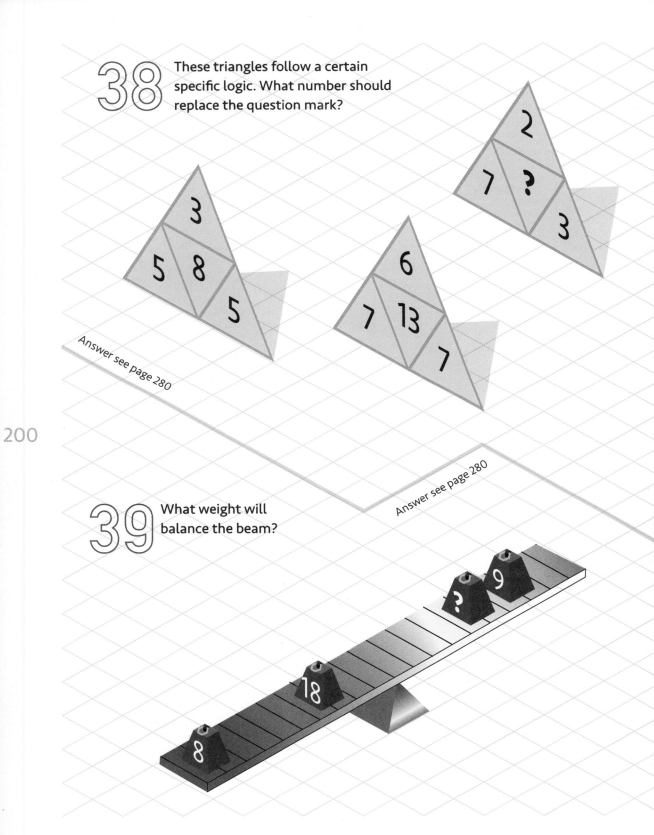

38 These triangles follow a certain specific logic. What number should replace the question mark?

2
7 ? 3

3
5 8 5

6
7 13 7

Answer see page 280

Answer see page 280

39 What weight will balance the beam?

9
?
18
8

These numbers, when placed correctly into the grid, will give you two numbers which are multiples of the number 84337.

Can you disentangle them?

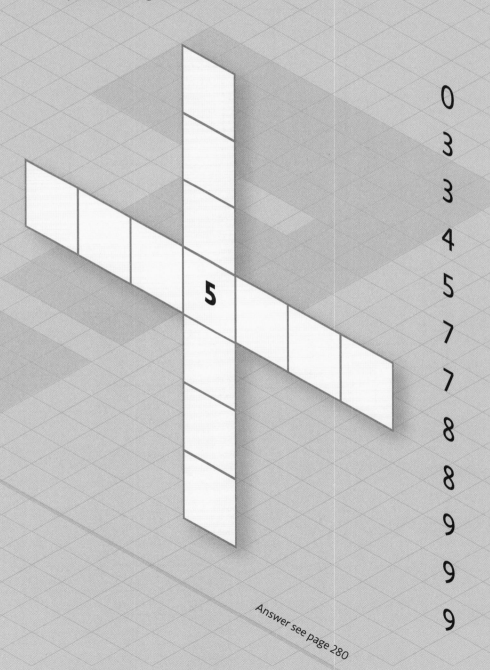

0
3
3
4
5
7
7
8
8
9
9

201

Answer see page 280

Which of the four options A-D below most closely matches the conditions of the top figure?

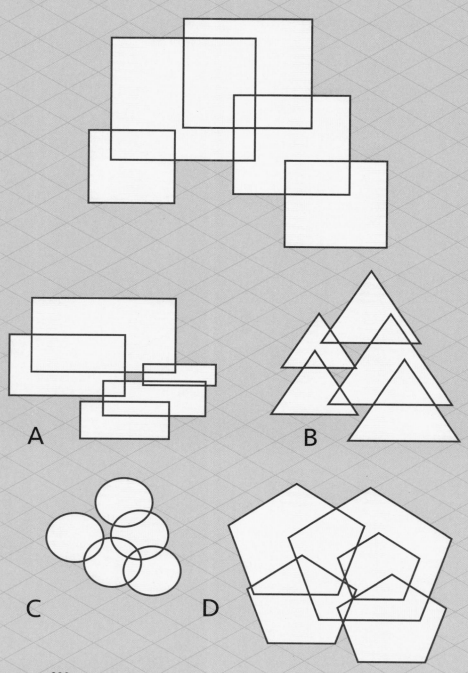

A

B

C

D

Answer see page 280

42 Which of the shapes below, A-E, fits with the shape above to form a perfect dark octagon?

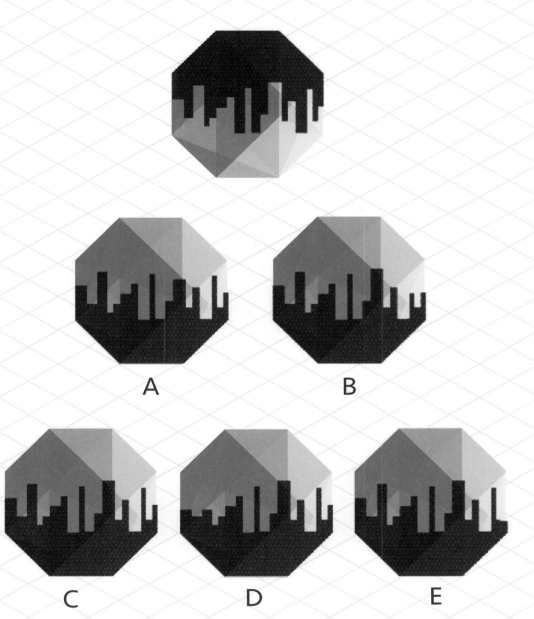

A

B

C

D

E

Answer see page 280

Several famous paintings have been encoded using the key below. Can you decipher them?

1	2	3	4	5	6	7	8	9
a	b	c	d	e	f	g	h	i
j	k	l	m	n	o	p	q	r
s	t	u	v	w	x	y	z	

7	9	3	1	5	7	7	5	9	1	9	3	9	4	2	6	3	4	6	9	2	8	5	9	6	9	9	5	
4	1	6	9	2	5	3	2	4	1	5	5	9	1	3	2	6	9	1	9	2	9	9	7	2	7	3	8	
6	9	9	2	1	9	4	1	5	9	4	5	5	9	2	5	9	7	8	5	9	1	3	5	4	1	7		
6	9	1	5	3	9	1	3	6	9	7	6	7	1	9	3	1	9	5	9	4	1	3	9	1	3	5	5	5
4	9	5	3	5	5	2	9	4	1	5	9	7	6	7	8	9	1	5	3	6	7	6	9	2	9	1	9	2

Answer see page 280

Answer see page 281

Following the logic of this grid, what number should replace the question mark?

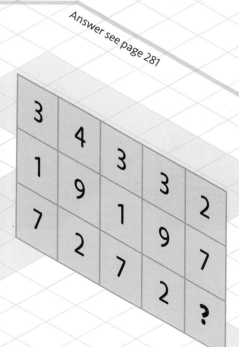

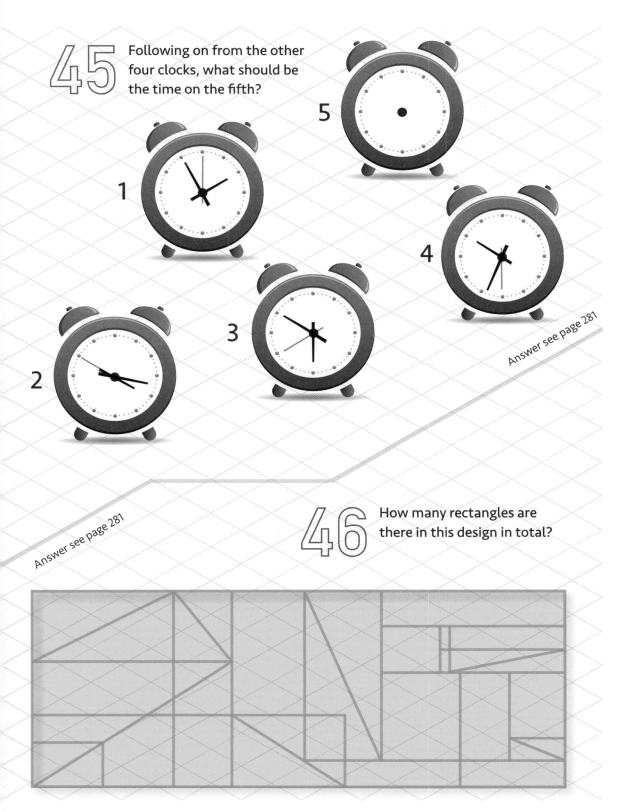

45 Following on from the other four clocks, what should be the time on the fifth?

5

1

4

3

2

Answer see page 281

Answer see page 281

205

46 How many rectangles are there in this design in total?

Signs – symbols in a specific position – which appear in the outer circles are transferred to the inner circle as follows: If it appears once or thrice, it is definitely transferred. If it appears twice, it is transferred if no other symbol will be transferred. If it appears four times, it is not transferred.

What does the inner circle look like?

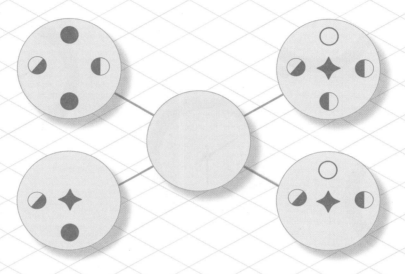

206

Answer see page 281

Starting at one corner and spiralling around to end on the centre square, you will find a nine-letter word. Two of the letters are missing. What is it?

Answer see page 281

49 The following list of numbers represents creatures whose letters have been encoded into the numbers needed to reproduce them on a typical phone dial.

Can you decode them?

Answer see page 281

262 266 32

424 7

324 436 2

783 892 5

268 328 37

50

Four of these five pieces fit together to make a regular geometric shape. Which one is left over?

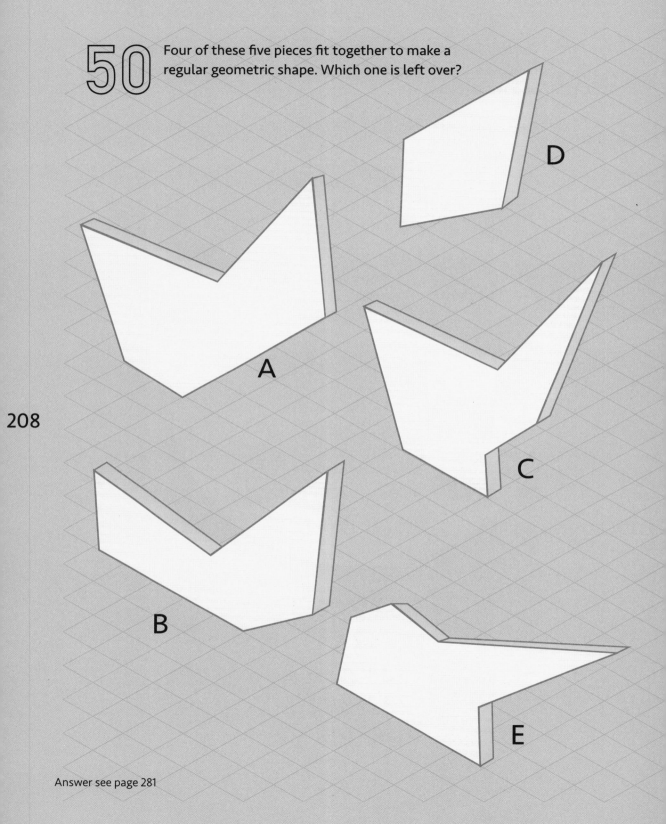

A

B

C

D

E

Answer see page 281

51 The following numbers obey a certain logic. What number should replace the question mark?

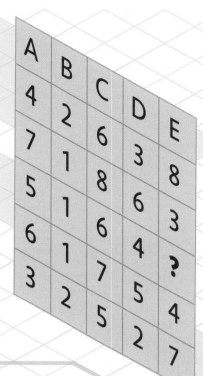

A	B	C	D	E
4	2	6	D	E
7	1	6	3	8
5	1	8	6	3
6	1	6	4	?
3	2	7	5	4
	5	5	2	7

Answer see page 281

52 The symbols in this design appear in a certain order. Which should replace the question mark?

Answer see page 281

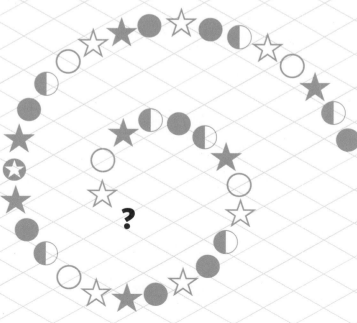

53

Which of these is the odd one out?

A: WILSON
B: DOUGLAS-HOME
C: ATTLEE
D: KINNOCK
E: ASQUITH

F: BALFOUR
G: MACDONALD

Answer see page 281

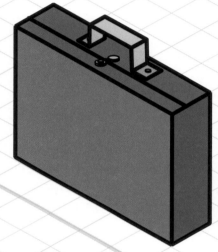

54

What is the missing number?

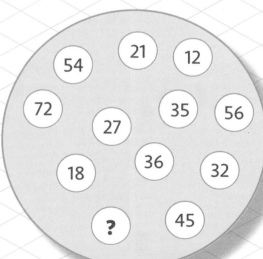

54 21 12
72 35 56
27
36
18 32
? 45

Answer see page 281

55 The numbers in this list are sequential terms in a specific sequence of numbers, but the numbers in the right hand column have been scrambled. What is the sequence?

1 3 3 3 4 4 4	5 5 6 7 7 7 7
1 3 3 3 4 5	5 5 7 7 8
1 3 4 4 4	6 6 6 6 7 7
1 3 4 5	6 6 7 7
1 4 5	6 6 8
1 6	7 7

Answer see page 282

Answer see page 281

56 What is special about the integer

8,549,176,320

that is not true of any other specific positive integer?

Answer see page 282

57 Which of the following numbers is not a numerical anagram of 93426151821685832045?

a. 12429311460825685538

b. 26484235258110396851

c. 35911246838860214552

d. 08926155228814465132

e. 89836550418215132426

f. 82563135415849680212

g. 35622882145386150941

h. 82563293615240158148

i. 56065134815221432988

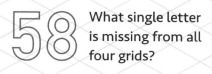

58 What single letter is missing from all four grids?

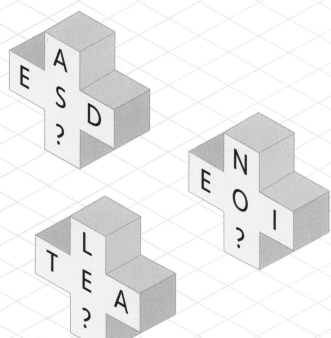

Answer see page 282

213

Answer see page 282

59 The following diagram operates according to a particular logic. Which letter should replace the question mark?

60

Logically, which letter does not belong in the second circle?

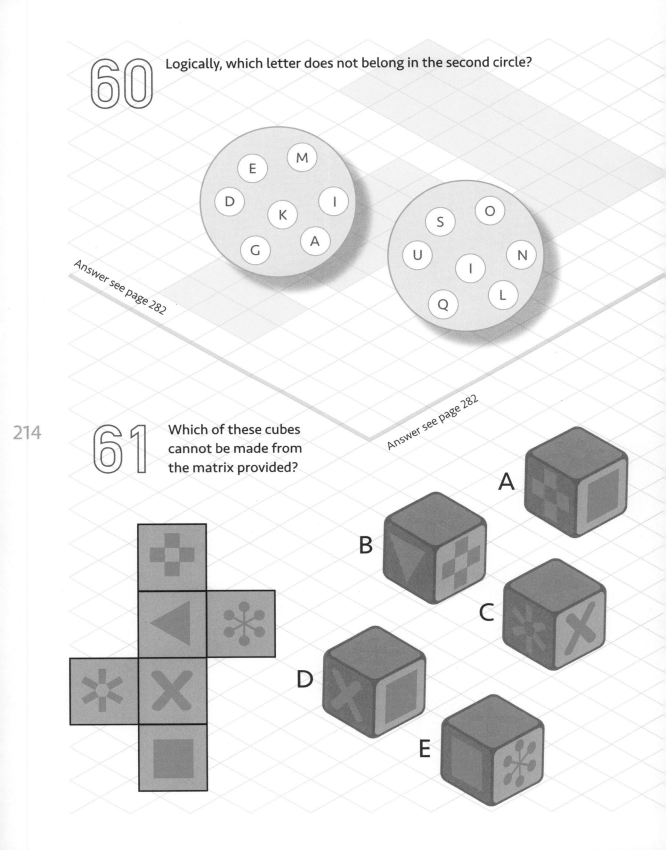

Answer see page 282

Answer see page 282

214

61

Which of these cubes cannot be made from the matrix provided?

A

B

C

D

E

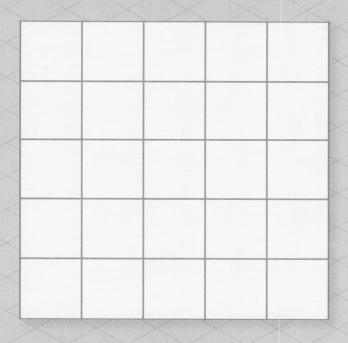

62

The following tiles have been taken from a five by five square of numbers. When they have been reassembled accurately, the square will show the same five numbers reading both across and down.

Can you rebuild it?

Tiles:

1 1 9

2 7 6

1 5 9

9 0 2 5 1 8

0 / 1 / 8

8 / 4 / 2

4 / 3 / 1

7 / 6

Answer see page 282

63

The dots on this grid have been filled according to a specific logic. One filled dot has been left out. Where should it go?

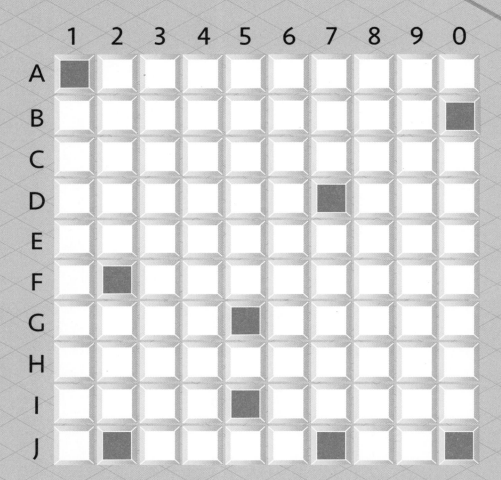

Answer see page 282

64

When the following grid is completed correctly, it will contain six different numbers that can follow 893 to produce a six-digit number that has 149 as a divisor.

Answer see page 282

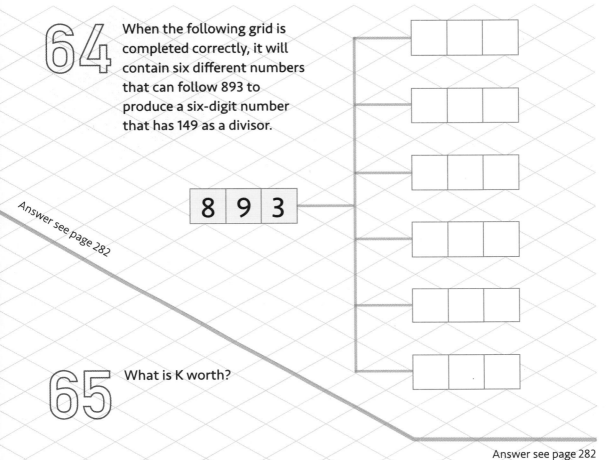

8 9 3

65

What is K worth?

Answer see page 282

217

$$K + K + N = 42$$
$$L + M + N = 34$$
$$K + M + N = 29$$
$$L + N + L = 52$$

66

If Amanda supports the Tigers, Bridget supports the Rhinos, and Taylor supports the Elks, who does Annie support?

a. The Leopards
b. The Bulldogs
c. The Human Beings
d. The Moose
e. The Antelopes

Answer see page 282

Answer see page 282

67

Each symbol in the grid has a consistent value. What number should replace the question mark?

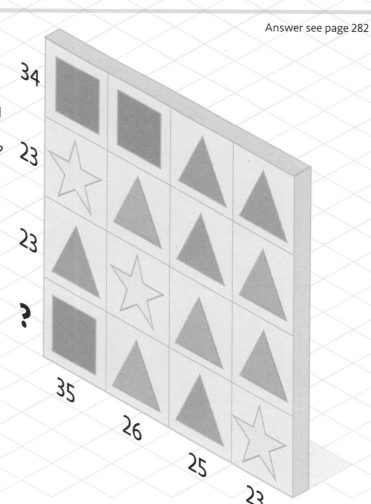

34

23

23

?

35

26

25

23

218

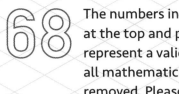

The numbers in this diagram, starting at the top and progressing clockwise, represent a valid equation from which all mathematical operators have been removed. Please add back in +, −, * and / signs as necessary to make the equation valid, evaluating each sign's result strictly as you come to it.

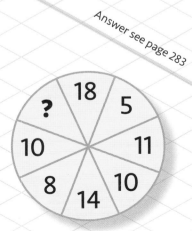

Answer see page 282

These circles function according to a certain logic. What number should replace the question mark?

Answer see page 283

70 One of the squares in the 3x3 grid is incorrect. Which one?

Answer see page 283

Answer see page 283

71 Which letter is one to the right of the letter four to the right of the letter one to the right of the letter two to the left of the letter two to the left of the letter immediately towards the middle of the line from the letter three to the right of the letter two to the right of the letter E?

A B C D E F G H I J K L

72 Using only numbers available in the grid below, subtract the largest Mersenne number (prime numbers that are one less than a power of two) from the number with the most divisors. What is the result?

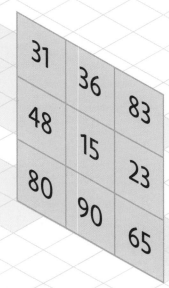

31	36	83
48	15	23
80	90	65

Answer see page 283

Answer see page 283

73 You have 56 biscuits to feed to your ten pets, which are made up of some cats and some dogs. Dogs get 6 biscuits, while cats get 5. You finish with one biscuit remaining. How many cats and how many dogs do you have?

74 Can you find the 36 numbers shown below within the number grid?

9	7	4	9	5	6	7	0	1	3	6	9	8	1	6
0	7	1	1	2	9	0	0	0	8	4	6	9	3	2
9	8	2	1	4	3	7	6	0	9	9	2	7	3	9
6	9	4	5	0	5	5	7	2	0	2	2	7	5	7
0	3	1	9	5	9	8	6	9	4	7	8	9	1	3
4	3	1	6	2	5	3	2	2	1	9	2	4	3	3
6	9	8	0	9	6	9	2	0	4	8	4	2	7	7
6	1	1	8	9	8	4	5	9	0	5	0	0	1	8
9	6	5	1	5	7	8	9	7	1	2	8	3	4	7
0	8	7	3	7	5	0	7	8	4	2	1	6	0	0
8	1	9	3	1	8	2	6	0	7	8	6	6	3	9
9	5	1	5	4	1	4	8	6	8	0	8	0	9	1
6	6	7	1	9	6	6	4	8	5	1	8	9	2	3
3	1	5	1	1	6	9	3	2	3	7	9	2	3	8
5	1	9	3	5	5	2	5	6	0	0	4	6	0	0

270	11513	525600	29122352
277	37926	789462	66406909
422	40392	968959	79420366
1377	68414	2143760	87091380
2048	69809	4660525	112900084
2258	75505	4802469	124118157
4898	180788	5193552	622824081
5962	351371	9853956	749567013
9927	488930	15148099	861933987

Answer see page 283

75

Which is the odd one out?

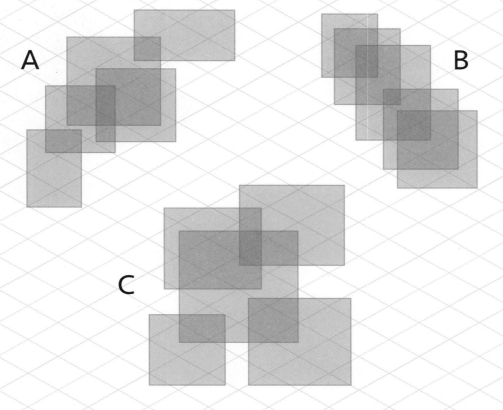

A

B

C

223

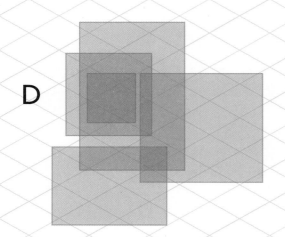

D

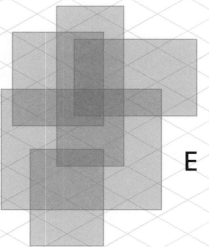

E

Answer see page 283

76

The following terms are all anagrams of mountains. Can you disentangle them?

CLONE TUMMY INK

OMAN JAIL IRK

AEROBIC ZIP ADO

TOP PEACE PLOT

DUB MACHINE

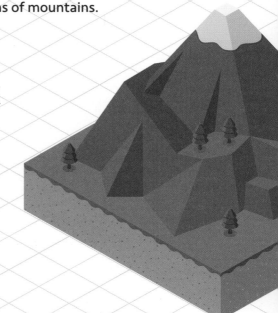

Answer see page 283

Answer see page 283

77

Either multiplying or dividing by a single-digit integer each time, and making sure each result is between 0 and 9999, can you get from the top number to the bottom number using precisely three intermediate steps?

1	3	4	4
1	9	6	0

Can you tell what number comes next in this sequence?

1 2 5 10 17 26 ?

Answer see page 283

Answer see page 283

79 Moving from circle to circle without backtracking, can you find a ten-digit square number that uses each digit once?

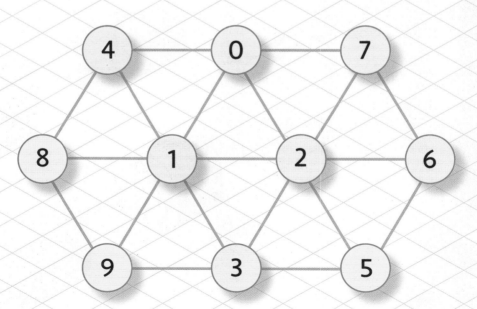

80

These pairs of circles obey a certain logic.
What letter should replace the question mark?

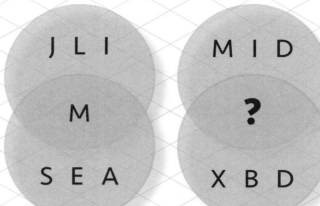

J L I

M

S E A

M I D

?

X B D

Answer see page 283

226

81

These suitcases are shown with their destinations. Which is the odd one out?

Answer see page 283

Australia

Corfu

Borneo

Dodecanese

Elba

82

Which trio of sides contain the same roman numbers?

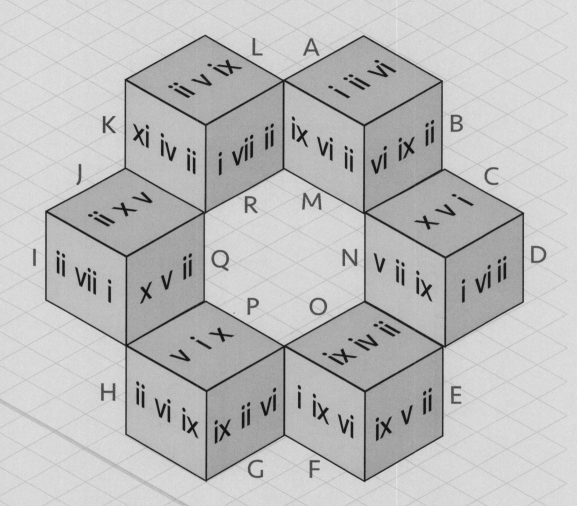

Answer see page 284

Six of these seven numbers are logically related.
Which is the odd one out?

28 14 55 46 82 64 41

Answer see page 284

Answer see page 284

Starting at any corner, follow the paths until you have five numbers, including the one where you started. Do not backtrack. Add the five together. What is the highest number you can obtain?

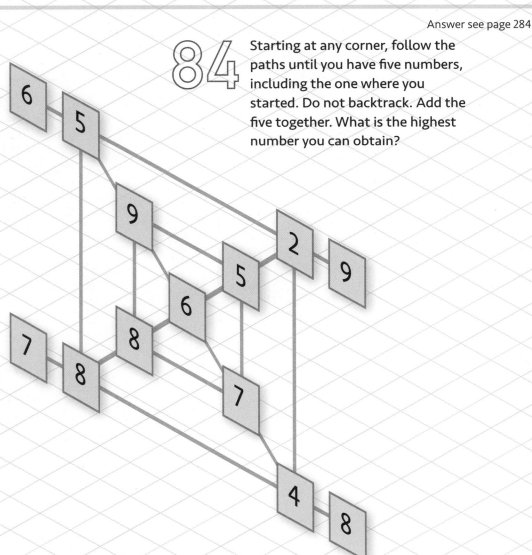

85

These rings obey a certain logic. What number should replace the question mark?

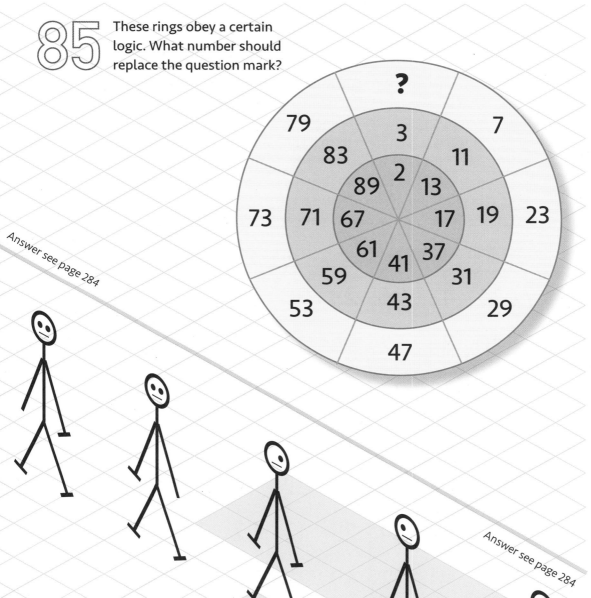

79 · ? · 7
83 · 3 · 11
89 · 2 · 13
73 · 71 · 67 · 17 · 19 · 23
61 · 37
59 · 41 · 31
53 · 43 · 29
47

Answer see page 284

86

What would the next matchstick person in this sequence look like?

Answer see page 284

87

Can you find the square which contains the number in this grid that is 3 squares from itself plus seven, 4 squares from itself minus thirteen, 5 squares from itself plus three, and 3 squares from itself minus two? All distances are in straight lines.

Answer see page 284

	a	b	c	d	e	f	g	h	i
1	14	48	96	28	98	74	41	40	92
2	40	84	52	95	17	84	25	29	65
3	85	18	77	20	28	54	81	22	7
4	17	86	9	30	84	67	20	56	80
5	29	55	4	66	32	17	29	60	11
6	33	18	84	25	12	52	78	41	61
7	36	41	12	49	20	70	12	24	98
8	57	27	89	94	25	35	64	22	12
9	75	58	35	61	23	83	39	52	68

Can you arrange the following twelve numbers into four groups of three related numbers each?

44   121   421

100   144   440

101   211   441

111   222   444

Answer see page 284

Answer see page 284

The following design works according to a certain logic. What number should replace the question mark?

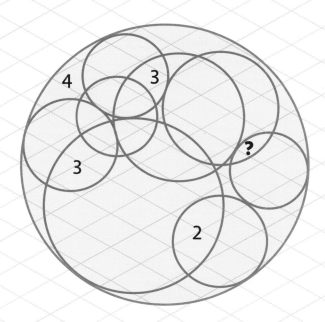

90

The following five items are all famous lakes. Can you decrypt them?

BDYNARXA   NARN

VRLQRPJW   XWCJARX

QDAXW

Answer see page 284

Answer see page 284

91

This non-pandigital grid obeys a certain logic. What number should replace the question mark?

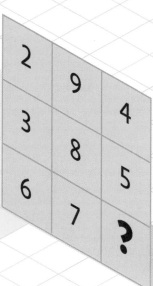

2		9
3		4
6	8	5
	7	?

92

This design follows a specific logic. What should replace the question mark?

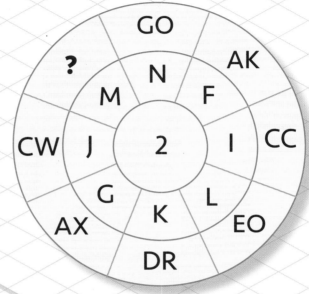

Answer see page 284

Answer see page 284

93

The letters and numbers in this square obey a certain logic. What number should replace the question mark?

94 According to the logic of these diagrams, what should replace the question mark?

Answer see page 284

95 There is a similarity between the two circles. Knowing that, what number should replace the question mark?

Answer see page 285

Answer see page 285

96 How many circles are in this congeries?

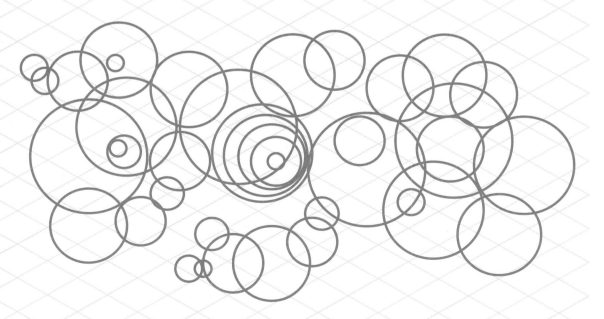

97

Which of the following is not an anagram of a type of cheese?

FOR TORQUE

YOWLS MELD

BATCH MINER

MEMBER CAT

NEWLY-SEALED

RICE LED RESET

Answer see page 285

Answer see page 285

98

Four 4-digit square numbers are jumbled in this square. Which pair of numbers is not used?

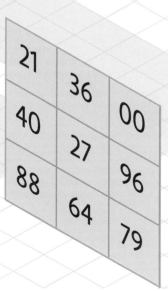

21		
36		
40		00
	27	
88		96
	64	
		79

Figure A is to figure B as figure C is to which figure?

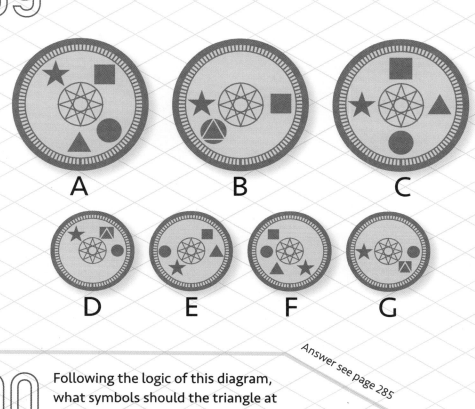

Answer see page 285

Following the logic of this diagram, what symbols should the triangle at the top contain?

Answer see page 285

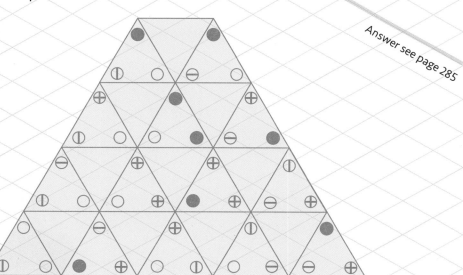

101

The numbers in this list are sequential terms in a specific sequence of numbers, but they are out of order. What is the sequence?

999999999989

9973

99999999977

99999989

99991

9999999967

9999999999971

999983

999999937

9999991

Answer see page 285

238

Answer see page 285

102

Given the five equations below, what is the value of x?

1. $3x^2 - x = b(ca + 2yb)$

2. $4b / 3 = c$

3. $a - x = c - by$

4. $(2x / 3)c = 2a + 2y$

5. $x + y = ay$

103

The word LUMINOUS is located exactly once in the grid below, but could be horizontally, vertically or diagonally forwards or backwards. Can you locate it?

Answer see page 285

239

```
O S N S I O M S S I O N I U I
L U S U M U N U S U L U U O N
M U N O I S N U M L U S L N S
S O I S U O O L U N S L S O I
I U U L M U L U M I U L S U N
L M S U M N M N U S I S M I O
S N U I N I I S I M L O M U S
I M I U I U L O U L I L M O N
I N O O S U O N I M U L S N N
M U O N U L O O U U U O L M U
O N U S I U L O M S M S N I L
L U M U U I S M L I U N M O L
L O U M M I S I U N U S S S I
I L N O O I O L O O S L N M O
N N L L I L S O O M S U U O I
```

104

In the following diagram, what number should replace the question mark?

Answer see page 285

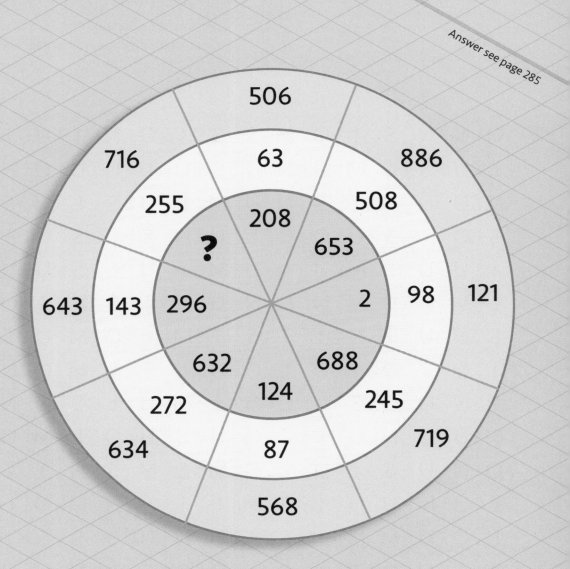

105

Can you work out the answer to this quick riddle?

What gets wetter the more it dries?

Answer see page 285

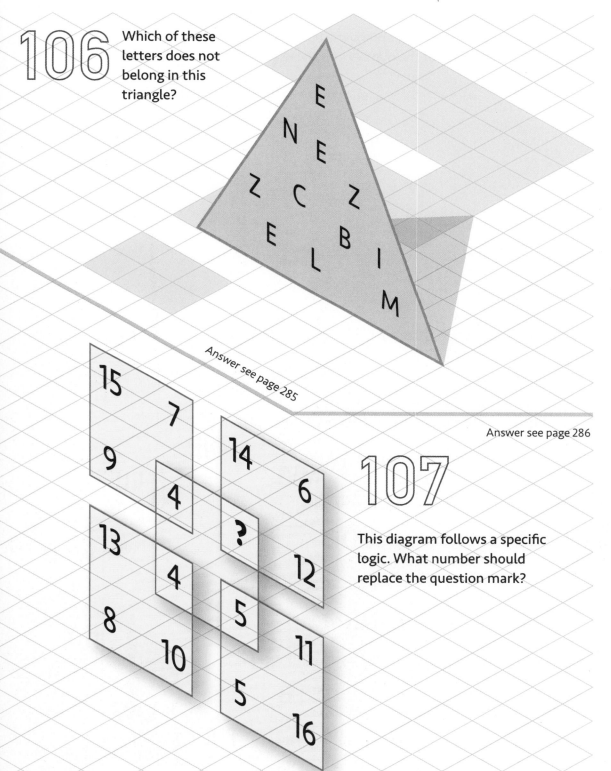

106 Which of these letters does not belong in this triangle?

E
N E
Z C Z
E B
L I
M

Answer see page 285

Answer see page 286

107

15
7
9
4
13
4
8
5
10

14
6
?
12
5
11
5
16

This diagram follows a specific logic. What number should replace the question mark?

108

Find a three-digit number which divides, using only whole numbers, into each of the numbers on the left.

33535

313111

73777 ☐ ☐ ☐

29299

3883

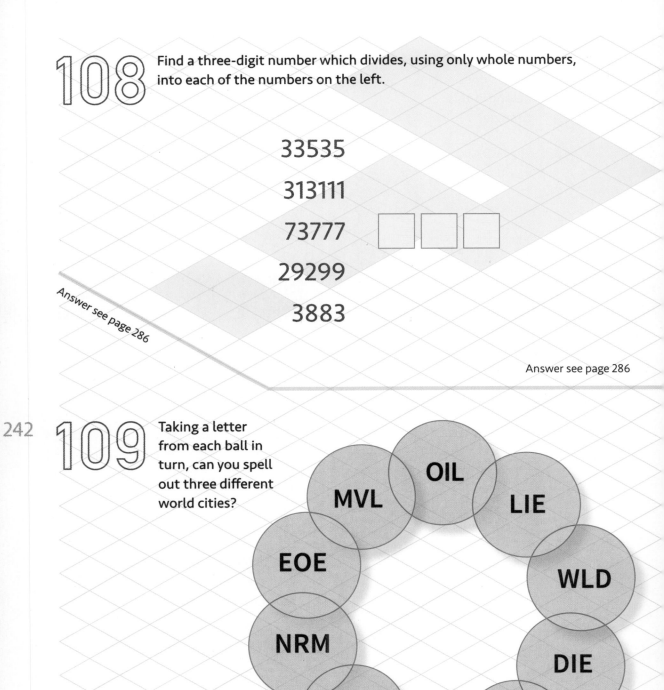

Answer see page 286

Answer see page 286

109

Taking a letter from each ball in turn, can you spell out three different world cities?

OIL
MVL
LIE
EOE
WLD
NRM
DIE
STB
LAV
TIE

110 Take one letter from each bulb in turn to find five rivers. What are they?

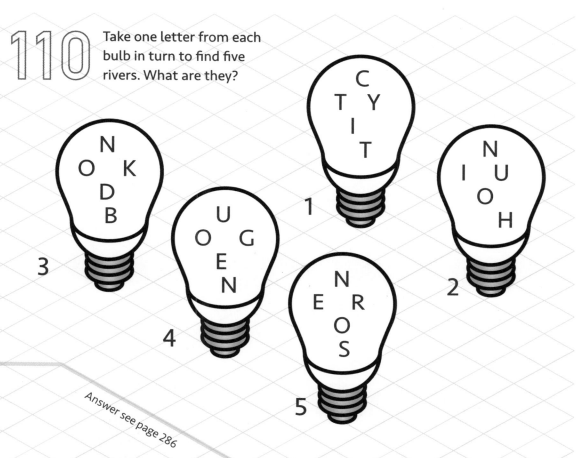

1

2

3

4

5

Answer see page 286

Answer see page 286

111 A committee of five needs to be drawn from twelve people, five men and seven women. There must be at least two women and one man. How many different ways of doing this are there?

112

There is a pattern behind these dominoes. What should replace the question mark?

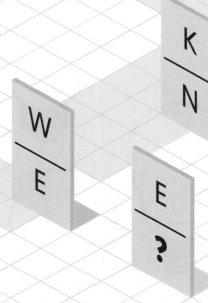

K / N

O / T

W / E

E / ?

Answer see page 286

Answer see page 286

113

There is something wrong with this list. Can you tell what it is?

Biscay   Baffin

Chesapeake   Bengal

James   Fundy

Hudson   Campeche

Ionian

Can you find your way through this maze?

START

FINISH

245

Answer see page 286

EASY ANSWERS

01

Haiti, Ibiza and Bali.

02

26 minutes and 40 seconds.

03

Five. On each row the first two-digit number, minus the next number, gives the last two-digit number.

04

Multiply, minus, plus and divide.

05

15:30 or 3:30pm.

06

40 using minus, divide, plus and multiply. **Minus 8** using divide, plus, minus and multiply.

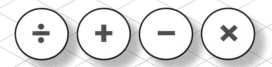

07

Four. Each square totals 21.

08

25. The alphabetical values of the two letters are added together.

09

Eight.

10

23:00 or 11pm.

11

7. Columns total 15, 20, 25, 30 and 35.

12

Vanished.

13

110.

14

4. The gap between the two alphabetical values gives the number.

15

Three. In each square multiply the two bottom numbers to get the two top numbers.

16

6. The number of straight lines in the letters are added or subtracted as stated.

17

Two. Plus, multiply, minus, divide and minus, plus, multiply, divide.

18

444 mph.

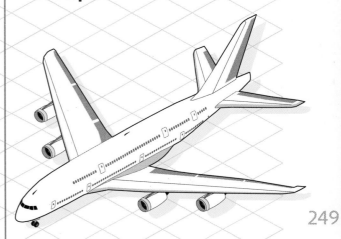

19

1. Add together the alphabetical values of the first two letters and subtract the third letter to give the number.

20

27.

21

4²/₃.

22

Eight.

14 + 4 + 4

10 + 6 + 6

10 + 10 + 2

8 + 8 + 6

14 + 6 + 2

12 + 8 + 2

12 + 6 + 4

10 + 8 + 4

23

No, it will be half a gallon short.

24

120. The numbers are 1x3, 2x4, 5x7, 6x8, 9x11, (10x12), ie., multiplying the next unused odd, or even, pair.

25

33.

```
                    85
              33        52
          12      21        31
      5       7       14        17
  3       2       5       9       8
```

26

840 mph.

27

466.

28

6 minutes and 15 seconds.

29

Three.

50 + 10 + 10

50 + 15 + 5

25 + 25 + 20

30

16 of each of 1¢, 5¢, 25¢ and $1.

31

6.5

32

92.5

33

310. The numbers increase by 20, 40, 60, 80 and 100.

34

Yes, with 0.2 gallons to spare.

35

1.25 gallons.

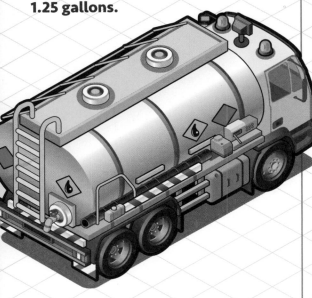

36

73. The two previous numbers are added together each time.

37

E.

38

96.1111

39

24.

40

One. The numbers are divided by 3, then 6, then 9, then 12.

41

250.

```
                    487
            250         237
        132       118        119
    79        53        65        54
55        24        29        36        18
```

42

185.

43

65 and 18.
Row 1: Box 1 x 20 = box 2,
box 1 + 20 = box 3
Row 2: Box 1 x 15 = box 2,
box 1 + 15 = box 3
Row 3: Box 1 x 10 = box 2,
box 1 + 10 = box 3
Row 4: Box 1 x 5 = box 2,
box 1 + 5 = box 3

44

South. A repeating sequence of
arrows pointing south, west, east,
north, south, west runs along the
top row and returns along the
second row and so on.

45

North. A repeating sequence of arrows
pointing north, west, east and south
runs down the first column and up
the next column and so on or, along
the top row and returning along the
second row and so on.

46

15000. Multiply by 20, then 15, then 10,
then 5.

47

2025. The alphabetical value of the
first letter gives the first two digits
and the alphabetical value of the last
letter gives the last two digits.

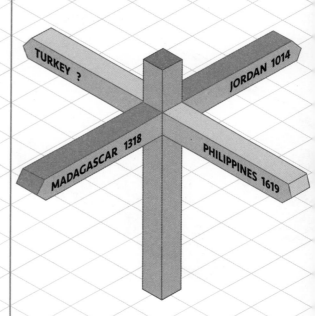

TURKEY ?
JORDAN 1014
MADAGASCAR 1318
PHILIPPINES 1619

48

4.

49

40. Add 2, add 4, add 6, add 8, add 10 etc.

50

31.

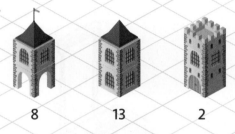

8   13   2

51

28 minutes and 45 seconds.

52

One. Moving clockwise along each edge, the alphabetical value of the first letter minus the alphabetical value of the second letter gives the number in the corner.

53

F. The alphabetical values of the two outer letters are added to give the value of the centre letter.

54

Cheese, ham, pickles, pastries, curries, samosas and salads. The reverse order is also valid.

55

88.

```
                    199
              111        88
          62       49        39
      34       28       21       18
   24       10       18        3       15
```

56

259. Multiply the first and second digits to get the third digit in each group.

57

90. The numbers are 1x2, 3x4, 5x6 etc.

58

125.

North. A sequence of arrows pointing north, west, east, south, east and west runs along the top row and repeats along the second row and so on.

105.

Multiply, plus, minus and divide.

Six. Each side of the triangle totals 18.

2 miles west.

B. (Initial letter of the location is the fourth letter of the name.)

63 (= 17+12+17+17).

022, 185, 348, 511, 674, 837

Cardiff (The others are in England.)

Bee Gees, Saturday Night Fever. Whitney Houston, The Bodyguard. Pink Floyd, The Dark Side of the Moon. Celine Dion, Falling Into You.

1 honest and 99 corrupt.

70

a6

71

6	8	3	5	2
8	0	1	5	1
3	1	7	6	9
5	5	6	4	8
2	1	9	8	2

72

Bottom centre. (The central small cross should be orthogonal, not diagonal.)

73

74

Uganda, Australia, Czech Republic, Mexico, Scotland.

75

10. (2+2+3+3)

76

21*31 = 651

77

European capitals alternate with random cities, but **Frankfurt is not the capital of Germany**; it should be Berlin.

78

Potassium. Manganese. Molybdenum. Phosphorus. Hydrogen.

79

Copenhagen, Georgetown, Bratislava

80

The **2L** tile that's in row 2 and column 3, where 1,1 is the top left corner.

81

W (sequence skips 2 letters, then 1, then 0).

82

Weapons: flamberge, guisarme, chakram. **Languages:** Ablaite, Palaic, Ugaritic.
Colours: Amaranthine, celadon, sanguineous.
Fish: barbel, snook, rasbora.

83

2. The 'true' sequence is the top row + first digit of second row: 1 5 3 7 2 6 4 8 0 9.

84

12 (L=13, M=17, N=11).

85

1. (Number of rectangles enclosing value)

86

T (Triangulated).

87

Manhattan, The Bronx, Brooklyn, Queens, Staten Island.

88

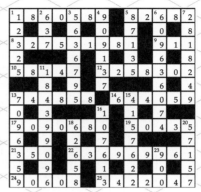

89

90

0.

91

PE. (Puli, Tosa, Skye, Chow)

92

4. (H=8, D=4, 8-4=4)

93

R. (cigar, brink, crows, smart).

94

Z. (Outer = Middle + Centre).

95

Marrakesh.

96

6 days. (In six days, both moons will be at 72 degrees to their starting point, making a straight line.)

97

27	21	22	18	33
19	29	28	22	23
23	24	20	30	24
31	25	19	25	21
21	22	32	26	20

98

B. (The others were all battles of the American Civil War).

99

G.

100

5 (Total=35).

101

D. (It has the two boxes overlapping by one corner each, with the circle overlapping an adjacent corner.)

102

D. (Whizzbangs)

103

An orange square.

104

105

D. (It is the only one containing shapes with no straight lines.)

106

1154 (*6, *17, *235, *12, *3, *21).

107

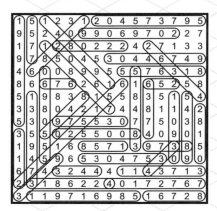

108

H. (The gap between letters increases by one each time.)

109

45.

110

F.

111

D.

112

3059056 and **3719534**.

113

Fortification.

114

5. 'X' = 5, 'Y' = 3, 'Z' = 9.

115

Pings Hip (shipping). Others are **dinheiro** (Portugal), **drachma** (Greece), **guilder** (British Guiana), **koruna** (Czech Republic), **ostmark** (East Germany).

116

117

7.

118

E.

119

Powers of 5 (5^9 to 5^18).

120

761 (*47, *4, *476, *19, *9, *158).

121

6 (each segment totals 21)

122

792.

123

42 (=9+9+9+7+8)

124

H.

260

MEDIUM
ANSWERS

01

190.

| 10 | 70 | 55 |

02

One third of a gallon.

03

One. In each square add the two bottom numbers to get the two top numbers.

04

19:00, or 7pm.

05

One. Moving clockwise from the top, the sector totals increase by one each time.

06

9 and 24. On each row, divide the first number by three to get the second number and subtract three from the first number to get the third number.

07

108⅓ miles.

08

2 minutes and 37.5 seconds.

09

Gym – 12, Swimming – 4 and Walking – 10.

10

190. Each star = 100, each triangle = 50 and each rectangle = 20.

11

Nine of each of 1¢, 25¢, 50¢ and $1.

12

496.25.

13

1N on the fourth row.

14

Five.
15 + 5 + 5
10 + 10 + 5
12 + 10 + 3
15 + 6 + 4
15 + 10 + 0

15

18.

2   5   9

16

35. Each number on the left has been multiplied by 3.5 to give the number on the right.

17

11⅓ gallons.

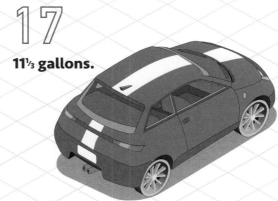

18

Six.

19

Four.
10 + 2 + 2
6 + 4 + 4
6 + 6 + 2
8 + 4 + 2

20

20.

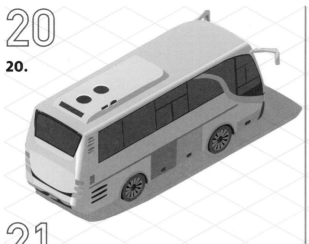

21

Monday
16th
Four
Wednesday

22

Two. On each row the first number plus the second number gives the last number and the third number plus the fourth number also gives the last number.

23

(17 + 13) ÷ 6 = √25

24

#. A sequence of #, %, $, £, ~, X runs down the first column and up the next and so on.

25

200 mph.

26

PAL. The value of each letter increases by one with each word.

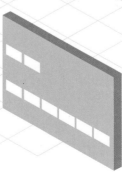

27

16. The alphabetical values of the first and last letter are added to give the number of miles.

28

2 on the top row and 6 on the bottom row. Add the top row of dashes to get the third box and multiply the bottom row of dashes to get the third box. (1+1 = 2, 3 x 2 = 6).

29

68 miles.

30

100. The total Roman numeral values give the number of viewers.

31

Three. Add the three top numbers to give the bottom two (8 + 3 + 2 = 13).

32

Two. On each row multiply the two outer numbers to give the two centre numbers.

33

24.

34

211.

```
                    474
              263       211
         146       117       94
      84       62       55       39
   60      24       38       17       22
```

35

23.00 or 11pm.

36

435.

| 85 | 100 | 125 |

37

8. The sum of the two outer numbers in each sector is placed in the centre of the opposite sector.

38

27. Add the middle number to each number in the top half then multiply by the middle number to get the number opposite.

39

90 and 21. On the top row multiply the first number by 3 to get the second number and add 3 to the first number to get the third number. On the next row multiply by 4 then add 4 to the first number and so on.

40

78.

```
                    175
              78          97
          30        48        49
      9        21        27        22
  8        1        20        7        15
```

41

1 minute and 15 seconds.

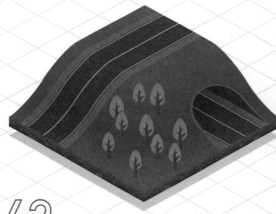

42

7. Opposite sectors total the same.

43

Three. The first digit minus the second digit of the left number, gives the number on the right.

44

80 and 38.
Row 1: Box 1 x 6 = box 2,
box 1 - 6 = box 3
Row 2: Box 1 x 5 = box 2,
box 1 - 5 = box 3
Row 3: Box 1 x 4 = box 2,
box 1 - 4 = box 3
Row 4: Box 1 x 3 = box 2,
box 1 - 3 = box 3
Row 5: Box 1 x 2 = box 2,
box 1 - 2 = box 3

45

46.

| 20 | 16 | 5 |

46

88 mph.

47

60. Add one to each number on the left and multiply by two to give the number on the right.

48

One hour and 12 minutes.

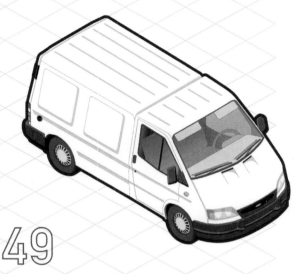

49

Two. Starting at the top of each group and moving clockwise, add the first three numbers and subtract the fourth number to give the fifth number. (2 + 5 + 4 − 9 = 2).

50

15. The alphabetical value of the last letter gives the number of miles.

51

D. Across each row (or down each column), dark circles subtract to give box 3, white circles add to give box 3.

52

12. Add together the two digits of each number on the left to give the answer on the right.

53

30 mph.

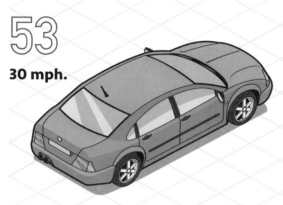

54

B. The triangle and square in the second and third lines of A, C and D have dark shading and the circles in the fourth lines of A, C and D feature dual shading.

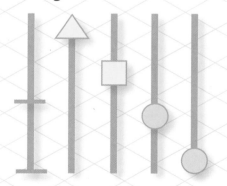

55

The figure would have **two hands and two feet**

56

P. (All letters represent the number of their position in the alphabet. Intersection is sum of top circle, difference between letters of bottom circle.)

57

A.

58

13. (Each number is equal to the sum of the two before it, starting with (0,1) as the initial pair. This is the Fibonacci sequence.)

59

1	●	●	2	●	1		1	●	1
	2			3				2	2
	1		●		●	2	2	3	●
	●	2		2			●	●	2
2	2	1	0			2			
●					●	2	1	●	●
	2	1	●		●	2		3	
●			1		2		1	2	●
●	3	2			●	2	2	●	3
2	●		●	2	1		●		●

60

4 (y=2, a=1, b=3, c=5).

61

10128233 (= 6703*1511), **27140447** (= 6703*4049), **52839749** (= 6703*7883).

62

2 * 16 lbs and 4 * 17 lbs.

63

Triangular Numbers.

64

Yellow triangle. (The centre symbol equal to one of the outer circles – in the first diagram, it is the bottom left symbol, and in each subsequent diagram, it advances one place clockwise round the circle.)

65

```
H S S P S I S H H S I I A S S
S S D D H I I A D P A A D S D
A I I A P D H S D A I A A P I
I A H P H A I A A A P D P P D
P D P H H I H D S D D H D I A
A P A S P I S I D P P D D A I
I P A I D I I A H I A I S I I
P I I I I A P D P I S H H P S
H A A P D A H I A A A P I H P
H D A S I I D D A I A P S P A
S A S S D A A S I S S S I H H
D A I P P S H I I S H S D S P
S D S D A I D I P D A S I D S
I A S A I I A A S I A I H P D
I P A S D P I D S S S P D I H
```

66

33. (Taking the letters as being worth a number equal to their position in the alphabet, increase the size of the gap to the next number by one each time.)

67

Dubai, Tomsk, Perth, Essen, Kyoto

68

0. (Second row subtracts from first row to give third row.)

69

8 (= 6 * 4 / 3)

70

19 (Add the two outer, horizontally adjacent numbers together, subtract the remaining outer number, and put the result in the inner cell of the diagonally opposite square.)

71

152843769, 412739856, 653927184, 735982641, 326597184.

72

$8 + 4 - 3 \times 2 - 7 + 5 - 9 = 7$

73

6 (E = The last digit of A+B)

74

● (After each repetition, the first two symbols are dropped)

75

35. (The others are prime)

76

Y. The first circle contains letters with horizontal symmetry.

77

4. (743-489=254)

78

Prime numbers.

79

11:25. (The hour hand goes back by two hours each time, and the minute hand forward by 25 minutes.)

80

A (rectangle)

81

B (The letters represent numbers based on their position in the alphabet, and in each row, the first column minus the second column equals the third column.)

82

1827049536.

83

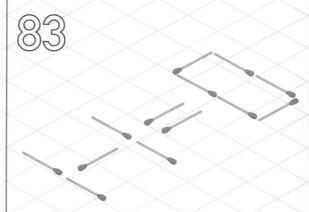

84

B. (Treating the letters as the numerical value of their position in the alphabet, in each column, the top row – the middle row = the bottom row.)

3 (In C, numbers from B are alternately doubled or halved.)

Our answer is (23 + 8 − 1) / 10 * 5 = (8 * 2) - 1.

i, n.

25. (Each number pairs with another to sum to 50.)

D. (Reading across, the second letter is as far past the first letter into the alphabet as the first was in from the start. So E > J, G > N, and B > D.)

One solution is 1024 *7 = 7168 / 4 = 1792 * 3 = 5376 / 2 = 2688.

30.

(next segment=) 576, (first prime<576=) 571, ((576-571)*5=) 25.

A5. The grid represents the numbers 1-100, and the dots are the prime numbers.

Fibonacci numbers (24th to 33rd in the sequence).

96

The 6D tile that's in row 1 and column 6, where 1,1 is the top left corner.

97

M. (Each circle is an 8-letter word backwards)

98

N. (The dominos contain the initial letters of the elements on the periodic table.)

99

Vera Cruz

100

22	33	16	35	9
34	9	21	31	20
30	18	38	8	21
12	20	30	17	36
17	35	10	24	29

101

5 (9-4=).

102

Square numbers.

103

3187 (*17, *54, *2, *26, *85, *23)

104

-14. (-2 + -5 + -2 + -5).

105

Flip twice. If you get either two heads or two tails, flip again. If you have one of each, assign H-T to one option, and T-H to the other. However biased it is, it will always have the same chance of generating T-H as H-T.

106

107

13. The 'true' sequence is: 638012503140.

108

10 and ²/₇ths days. (In 10 and ²/₇ths days, the faster moon will be at 51 and ³/₇ths degrees to its origin, having completed one circuit and started its second, whilst the slower moon will be precisely opposite the planet from it, at 231 and ³/₇ths degrees to its origin.)

109

Anna Karenina, Leo Tolstoy.

110

W ((2*18) + 2 – 15 = 23). Letters represent numbers in alphabetic position.

111

627953481, 847159236, 923187456, 215384976, 537219684.

112

A yellow square with a small blue square in the top right. (The 8-block pattern runs clockwise around the larger squares from top left, inverting tone and rotating one place counterclockwise after completion).

113

2. 'W' = 1, 'X' = 2, 'Y' = 4, 'Z' = 4

DIFFICULT ANSWERS

01

2.

3 2 5 1 4
1 4 3 2 5
2 5 1 4 3
4 3 2 5 1
5 1 4 3 2

02

Five. In each square multiply the two numbers on the right to get the two on the left.

03

Six and nine. In each square, the two top numbers are added to give the bottom left and multiplied to give the bottom right.

04

**Swimming – 27,
Boxing – 9**
and
Aerobics – 21.

05

G. The alphabetical value of the first letter, minus double the alphabetical value of the second letter gives the alphabetical value of the third letter.

06

Four. In each group, the sum of the two numbers on the left gives the top and the sum of the two numbers on the right also gives the top. (5 + 2 = 9, 4 + 4 = 8).

07

12 of each of 5¢, 10¢, 25¢ and $1.

08

34 minutes and 30 seconds.

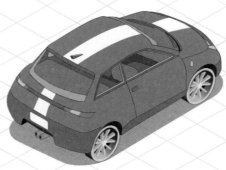

09

Three. On each row, the two-digit number on the left, minus the two-digit number on the right, gives the centre number.

10

A.

11

548. For each number, divide the second digit by the first to get the third.

12

35 using divide, plus, minus and multiply. **Minus 15** using divide, minus, plus and multiply.

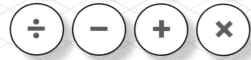

13

Divide, minus, plus and multiply.

14

530. All the other numbers are square numbers.

15

6 minutes and 7.5 seconds.

16

D.

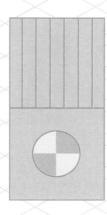

17

Six, each edge of the triangle totals 20.

18

Four.

19

91. A = 17, B = 24 C = 33.

20

85.

21

Italian – 8, Chinese – 2 and Indian – 7.

22

15. The numbers in the first group rise by eight each time, the numbers in the second group rise by six each time, the numbers in the third group rise by four each time and the numbers in the fourth group rise by two each time.

23

B.

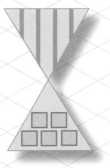

24

B.

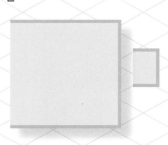

25

No, it will be 1.625 gallons short.

26

19.30 or 7.30pm.

27

Eight of each of 1¢, 5¢, 10¢ and 50¢.

28

A

29

C.

30

11.

31

Seven.

12 + 4 + 4

8 + 6 + 6

8 + 8 + 4

14 + 4 + 2

12 + 6 + 2

10 + 8 + 2

10 + 6 + 4

32

53. The number of consonants gives the first digit and the number of vowels gives the second digit.

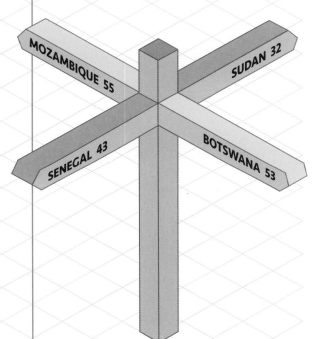

MOZAMBIQUE 55

SUDAN 32

SENEGAL 43

BOTSWANA 53

33

19. The numbers denote the alphanumeric positions of the first letter of the words one, two, three, four, and five (o = 15, t = 20 etc.) Six begins with s (19).

34

491. Pattern runs right then back left, from top left.

35

1	●		●	2		●	4	●		●	
	3	3	3	●	3	3	●	●	4	2	2
●		●			●	2				●	
●	●	3	3		2		1				
2			●	●				●		2	●
0			2	2		0	2	●	●		2
			1	1				2	3		●
1	●			●			0	0		●	●
2	3				1				3		
●	3	●	●	2			1	1	3	●	2
●			3	3	●			●	4	●	2
●		2	0		●	2	1		●	2	

36

1 (9761271 =*18664, 3913086=*7482, 1868679=*3573, 2504124 =*4788, 8013929 =*15323).

37

Our answer is ((13 + 5) * 6 + 4) / 16 = (6^2 – 8) / 4.

38

5 (2+3; the 7 is unused.)

39

12.6.

40

4975883 and **7505993** (*59 and *89).

41

B. (It is formed of five identically-shaped polygons of differing sizes which overlap each other but do not contain each other.)

42

C.

43

Giuseppe Arcimboldo, The Fire. Max Beckmann, Actors Triptych. Frits Van den Berghe, Sunday. Francisco Goya, Carnival Scene. Vincent van Gogh, Self-portrait

6. (Consider the second row as a single number, double it, and add it to the first row, also as a single number, to get the value of the entire third row.)

3:29 and 40 seconds. (The hour and minute increase each time by a regularly increasing amount, 1h 22m the first time, 2h 33m the second, and so on. The second hand increases by ten seconds.)

1298.

Regoliths

Anaconda, Ibis, Echidna, Quetzal, Anteater.

D (Six-pointed star).

5 (DE = AB - C, treating AB and DE as two-digit numbers).

◑ (When the pattern comes to the end of its cycle, it reverses direction.)

D. (The others were all prime minsters of the United Kingdom.)

20. (Each number groups with two others in forming the 3rd, 5th, and 8th multiple of a base number. 5*4 is missing.)

The RATS numbers, "Reverse Add, Then Sort", where to find each new term, you add the previous term to the number obtained by reversing the digits of that same previous term, and then you put the digits of the answer in ascending order – so 16+61 is 77. (5th to 17th in the sequence.)

56

It contains **all ten digits once**, in English alphabetical order.

57

D.

58

V (devas, breve, valet, ovine.)

59

L. (Treating the letters as the numerical value of their position in the alphabet, in each column, the top row of the previous column + the middle row of the previous column = the bottom row.)

60

N, which should be 'M'. Each letter in the second circle is 8 places further along the alphabet than a letter in the first circle.

61

B.

62

```
8   4   2   7   6
4   3   1   1   9
2   1   2   5   0
7   1   5   9   1
6   9   0   1   8
```

63

H5. (The grid represents the numbers 100 down to 1, and the dots are the squares.)

64

106, 255, 404, 553, 702, 851

65

0 (L=5, M=-13, N=42).

66

E. (Initial letter of the team is the final letter of the next person's name.)

67

29 (= 10+4+7+8).

68

9 * 7 – 18 / 5 + 23 * 2 / 8 = 8

69

4 (all three circles total to 80).

70

Centre left. (The unbroken mid-size circle is missing.)

71

I.

72

90-31=59

73

5 of each. (5*6)+(5*5)=(56-1)

74

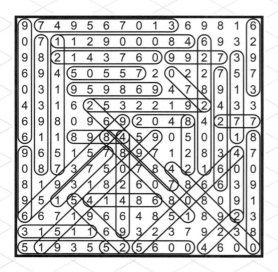

75

D. (It is the only one to have a box whose sides intersect no other sides.)

76

Mount McKinley, Kilimanjaro, Pico de Orizaba, Popocatepetl, Ben Macdhui.

77

One solution is 1344* 7 = 9408 / 3 = 3136 / 8 = 392 * 5 = 1960.

78

37. (The term increases, each time, by the odd numbers in increasing order, starting with 1.)

79

9814072356

80

R (13+9-4 = 24-2-4=18).

81

D. (The others are individual islands)

e, l, n

55. (The others form pairs in which each number is the other with the order of the digits reversed.)

38 (=7+8+8+9+6).

5 (The rings hold the prime numbers in order, from the centre of the upper left segment to the outer, then from the outer back to the inner of the second segment, and so on.)

The figure would be missing the right leg.

f3

Squares = 121, 144, 441; Primes = 101, 211, 421; Happy = 44, 100, 440; Divisors of 888 = 111, 222, 444

2. (Number of sides immediately surrounding value.)

Superior, Michigan, Huron, Erie, Ontario.

9 (679 – 385 = 294).

FN. (Converting letters into numbers, the outer circle is the middle circle to the power of the inner circle. The values of the outer circle are given as a form of base 26 that uses the letters A-Z as digits.)

9. (Clockwise from left, and replacing numbers with the letter in that position of the alphabet, the entries in the grid spell out RATIONALISTS.)

Yellow circle. (Add the number of sides of the symbols around the centre to find how many sides the central symbol should have. Solid symbols are positive, outline symbols are negative.)

95

5 (6228-2408 = 3820 = 7495-3675).

96

40.

97

Chambertin, a wine. (The cheeses are roquefort, lymsewold, camembert, wensleydale, and red leicester.)

98

27 (4096, 6400, 7921, 8836).

99

5.

100

101

Largest prime number of X digits (X = 4 to 13).

102

6 (y=1, a=7, b=3, c=4).

103

```
O S N S I O M S S I O N I U I
L U S U M U N U S U L U U O N
M U N O I S N U M L U S L N S
S O I S U O O L U N S L S O I
I U U L M U L U M I U L S U N
L M S U M N M N U S I S M I O
S N U I N I I S I M L O M U S
I M I U I U L O U L I L M O N
I N O O (S U O N I M U L) S N N
M U O N U L O O U U U O L M U
O N U S I U L O M S M S N I L
L U M U U I S M L I U N M O L
L O U M M I S I U N U S S S I
I L N O O I O L O O S L N M O
N N L L I L S O O M S U U O I
```

104

491. Working inwards, n – (n+1) = (n+2) Absolute.

105

A towel.

106

L. All the others possess at least one degree of symmetry.

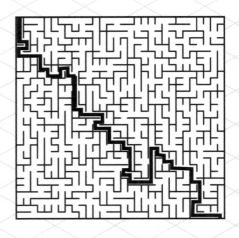

107

5 (Add the outer 3 numbers together, then add the digits of that result together to find the inner number.)

108

353 (*95, *887, *209, *83, *11).

109

Montevideo, Libreville, Willemstad

110

Congo, Indus, Yukon, Tiber, Rhone

111

735. (7!/2!5! * 5!/3!2! + 7!/3!4! * 5!/2!3! + 7!/4!3! * 5!/1!4!).

112

D. (The dominos spell out the word KNOTWEED.)

113

The Ionian is a sea. All the others are bays.

114

Puzzle Notes

Puzzle Notes